Vocal/Piano

Frank Sinatra
MORE OF HIS BEST
ORIGINAL KEYS FOR [SINGERS]

Cover Photo: JT / Retna Ltd.

ISBN 978-1-4234-8414-1

HAL•LEONARD®
CORPORATION
7777 W. BLUEMOUND RD. P.O. BOX 13819 MILWAUKEE, WI 53213

Visit Hal Leonard Online at
www.halleonard.com

ALL OF ME

Words and Music by SEYMOUR SIMONS
and GERALD MARKS

Take my lips, I want to lose _____ them. ___

_____ Take my arms; ___ I'll _____ nev-er

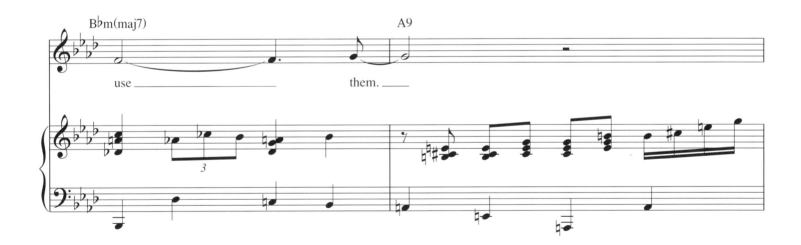

use _____ them. ___

Your _____ good - bye _____ left me with eyes ___

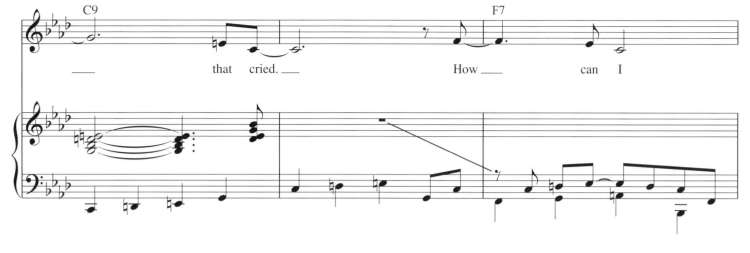

that cried. ___ How ___ can I

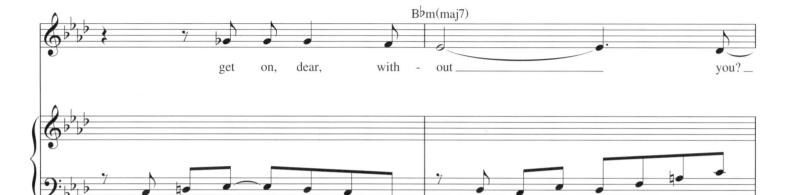

get on, dear, with - out _____ you? ___

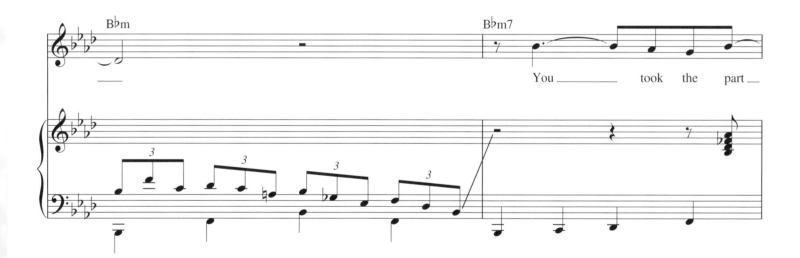

You _____ took the part ___

that once ___ was my heart, ___ so

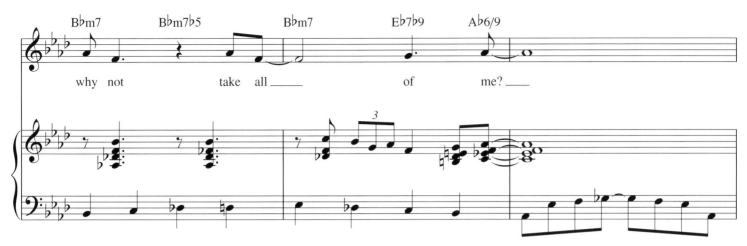

why not take all ____ of me? ____

All of me,

why not ____ take all of me? ____

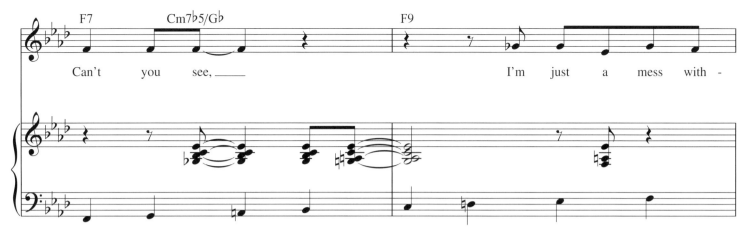

Can't you see, _____ I'm just a mess with -

out _____ you? _____ Take my lips;

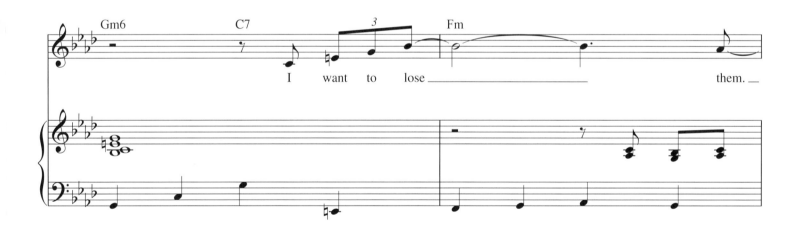

I want to lose _____ them. _____

_____ Why don't you take my arms; _____ I'll

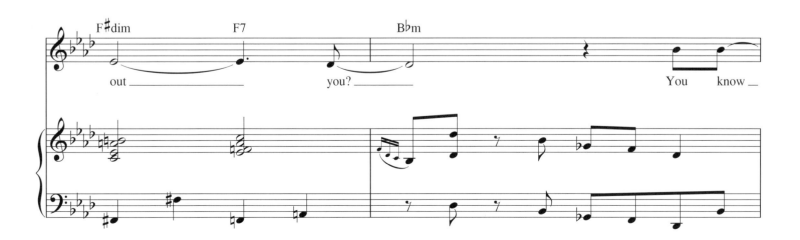

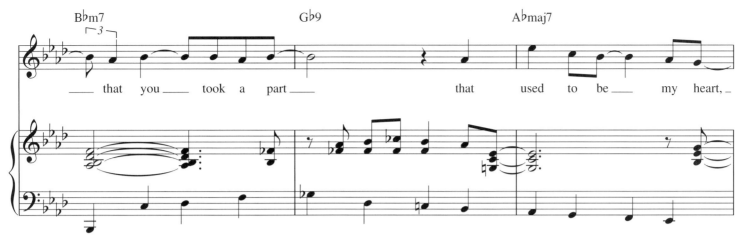

that you ___ took a part ___ that used to be ___ my heart, ___

___ so why not take all ___ of me? ___

Spoken: You'd better get it while you can, baby. *I'm leaving town pretty soon now.*

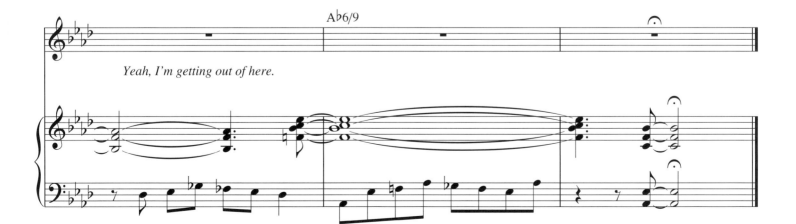

Yeah, I'm getting out of here.

ALMOST LIKE BEING IN LOVE

from BRIGADOON

Lyrics by ALAN JAY LERNER
Music by FREDERICK LOEWE

Moderately fast Swing

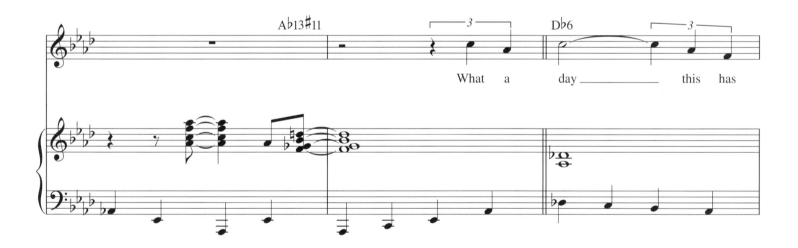

What a day _____ this has

been. What a rare _____ mood _ I'm in. Why, it's

al - most like ____ be - ing ____ in love. ____

There's a ____ smile on my face for ___ the

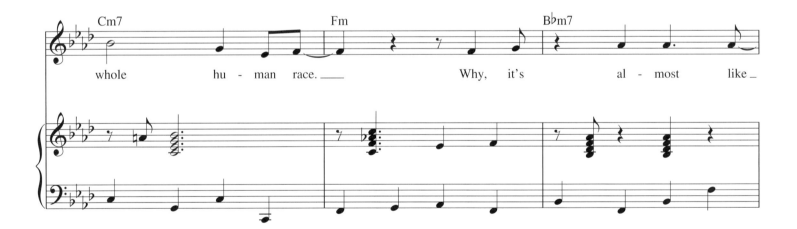

whole hu - man race. ____ Why, it's al - most like ____

____ be - ing ____ in love. ____ All the

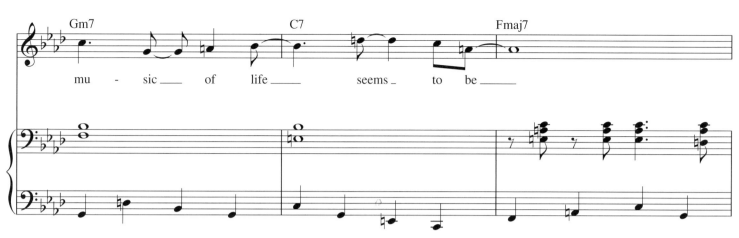

mu - sic ___ of life ___ seems ___ to be ___

like a bell _____ that is ring - ing ___ for

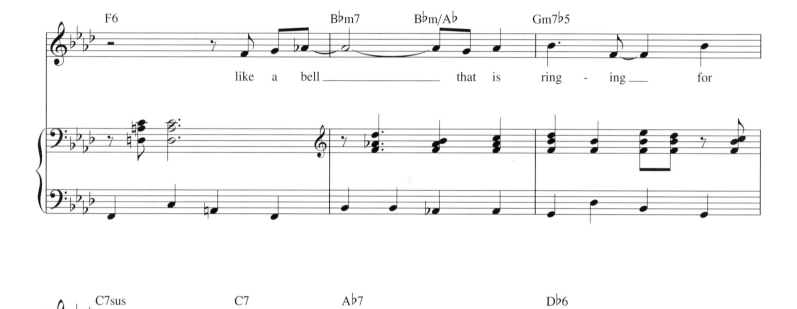

me. And from the way _____ that I

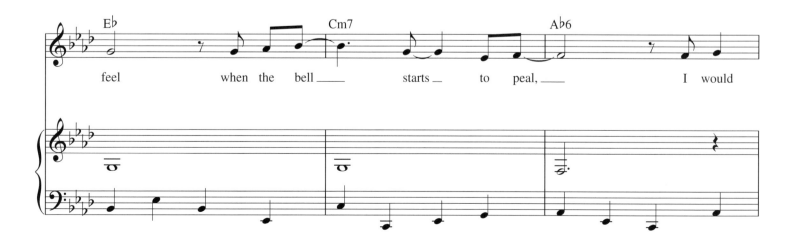

feel ___ when the bell ___ starts ___ to peal, ___ I would

swear I was fall - ing, I could swear I was fall -

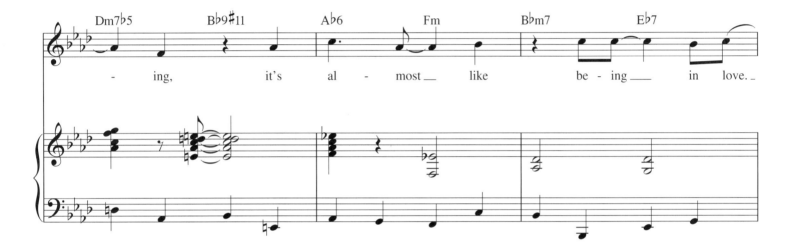

- ing, it's al - most __ like be - ing __ in love. __

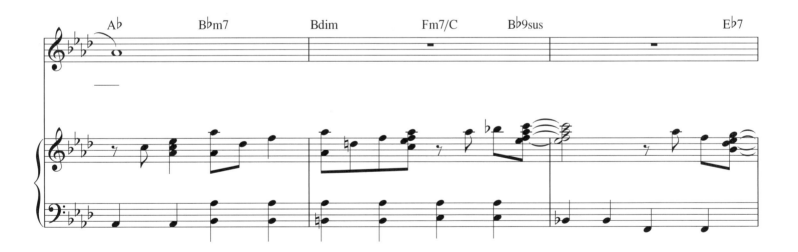

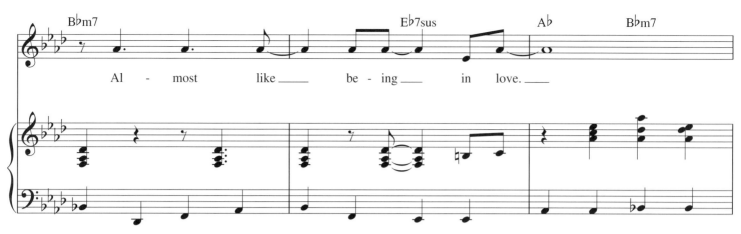

Al - most like ____ be - ing ____ in love. ____

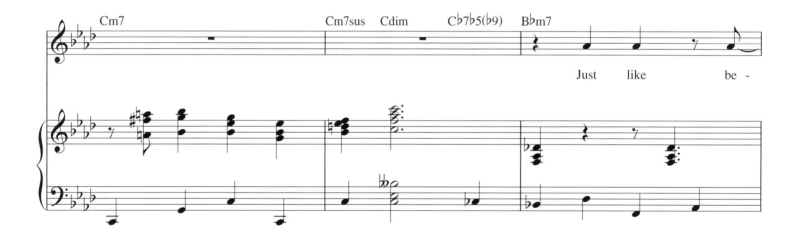

Just like be -

- ing in love. ____

All ____ the

Gm7 — Gm6 — C7sus2 — C7 — Fmaj7

mu - sic   of life ___ seems _ to be ___

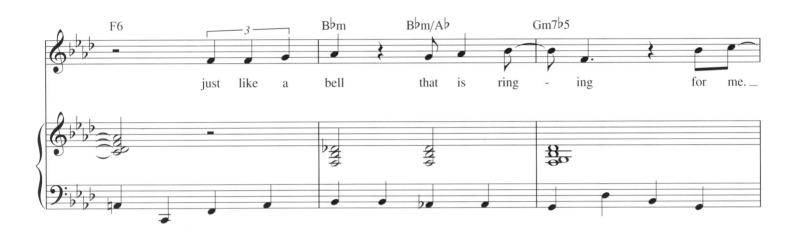

F6 — B♭m — B♭m/A♭ — Gm7♭5

just like a bell   that is ring - ing   for me. _

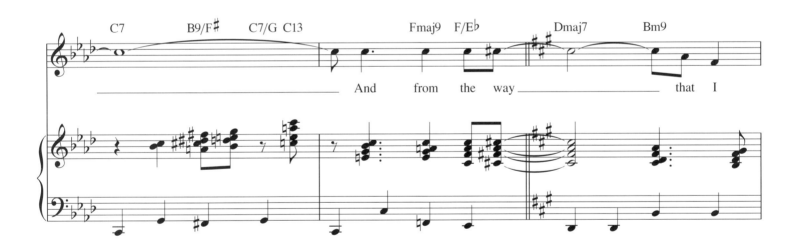

C7 — B9/F♯ — C7/G C13 — Fmaj9 F/E♭ — Dmaj7 — Bm9

___ And   from the way ___ that I

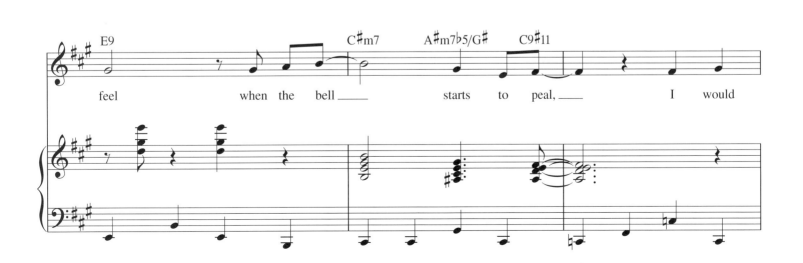

E9 — C♯m7 — A♯m7♭5/G♯ — C9♯11

feel   when the bell ___ starts to peal, ___ I would

swear ____ I was fall - ing, I could swear ____ I was

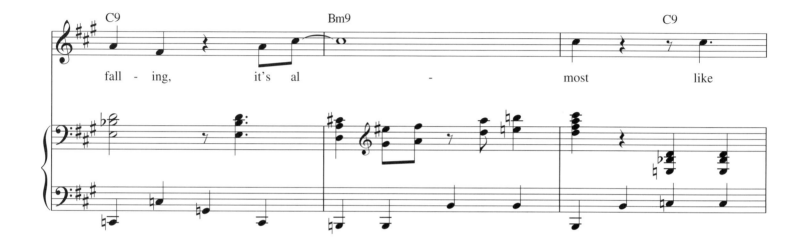

fall - ing, it's al - most like

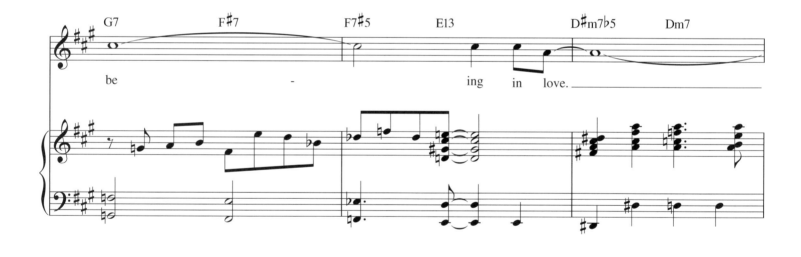

be - ing in love. ____

CHANGE PARTNERS
from the RKO Radio Motion Picture CAREFREE

Words and Music by
IRVING BERLIN

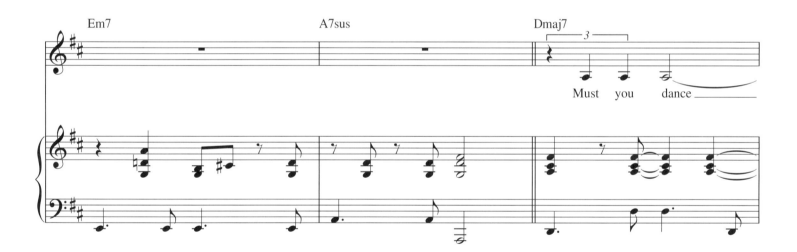

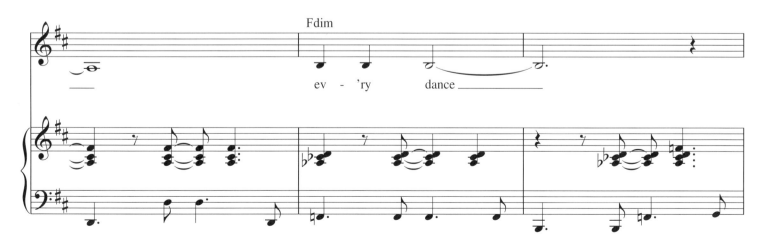

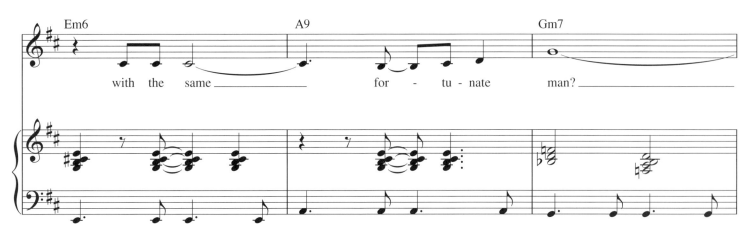

with the same _____ for - tu - nate man? _____

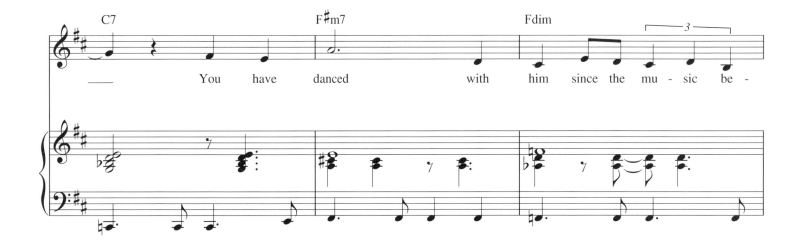

_____ You have danced with him since the mu - sic be -

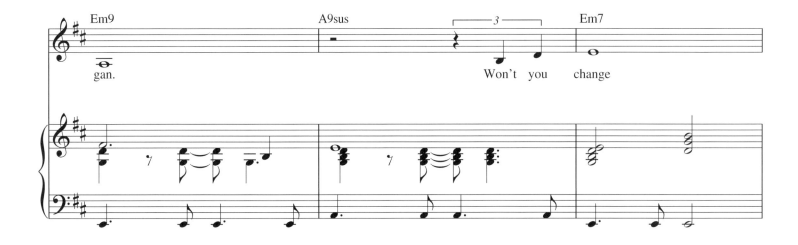

gan. Won't you change

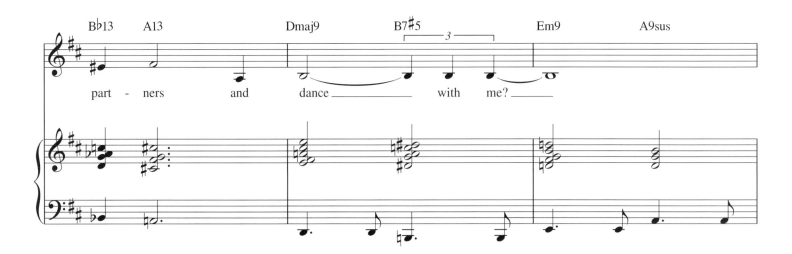

part - ners and dance _____ with me? _____

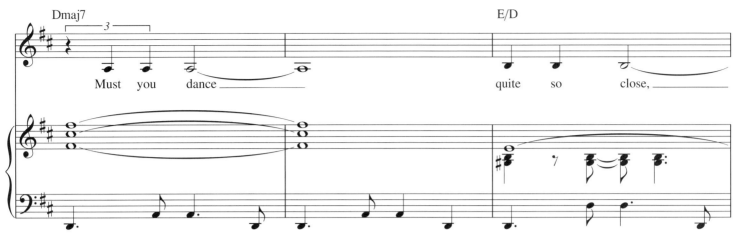

Must you dance _____ quite so close, _____

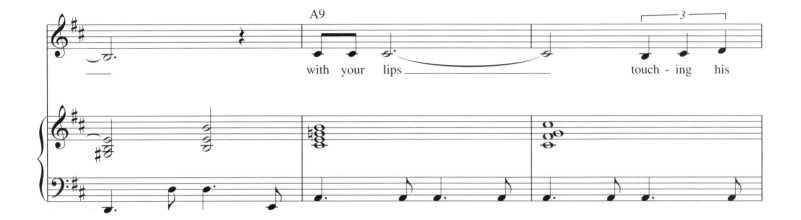

_____ with your lips _____ touch - ing his

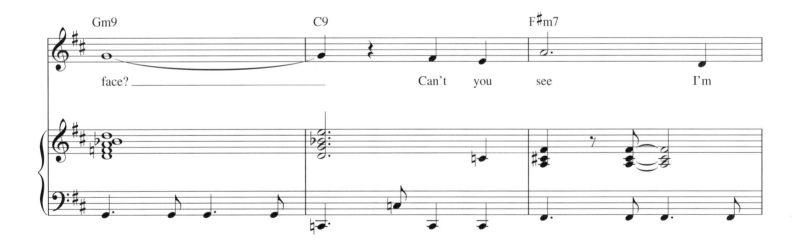

face? _____ Can't you see I'm

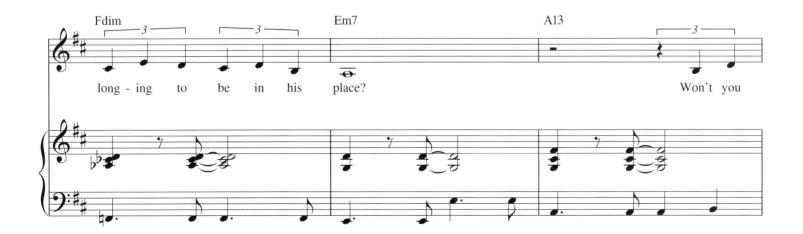

long - ing to be in his place? Won't you

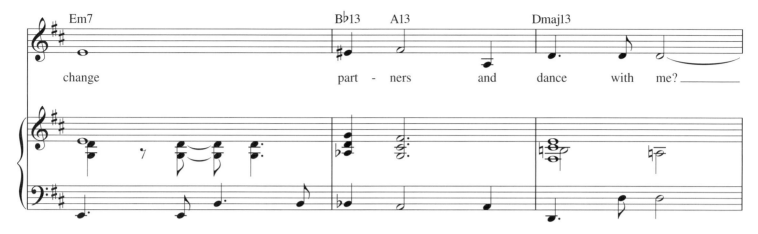

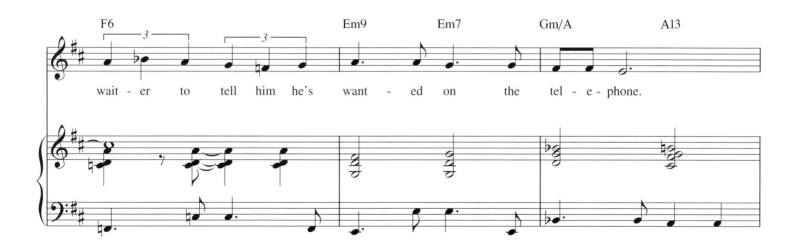

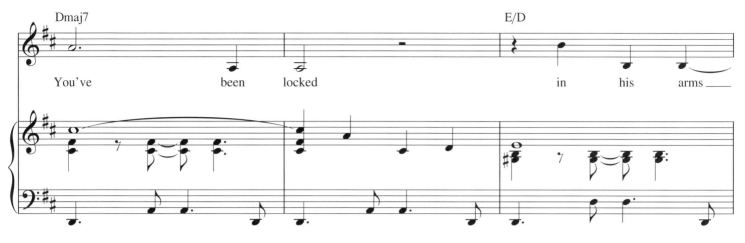

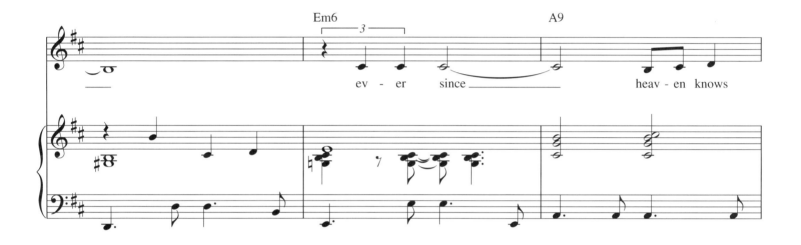

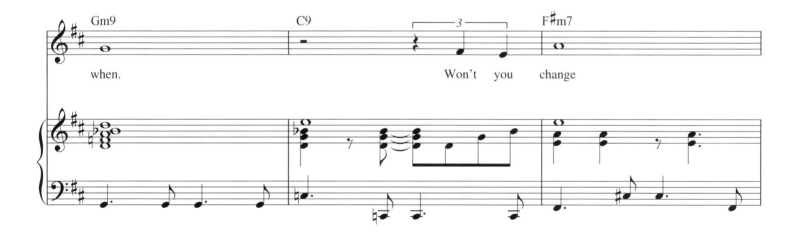

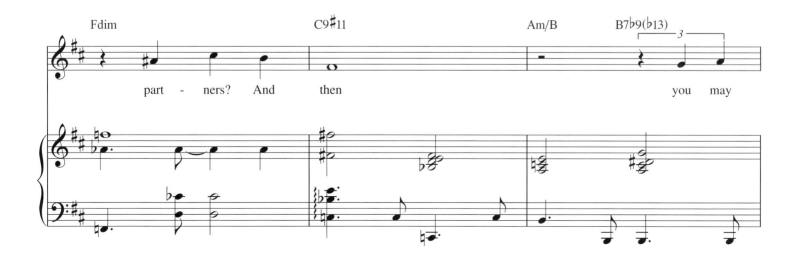

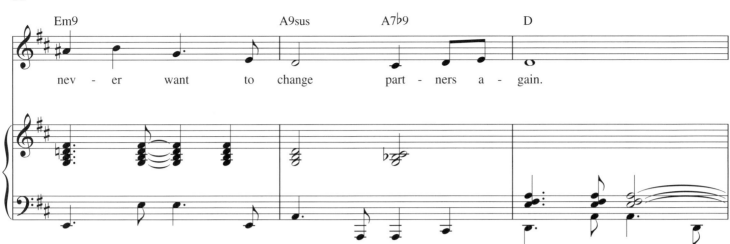

nev - er want to change part - ners a - gain.

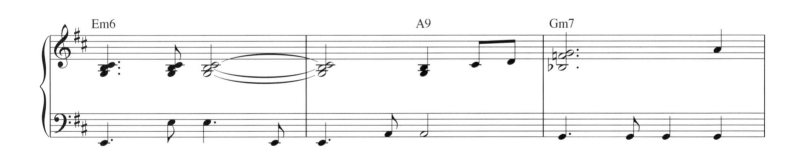

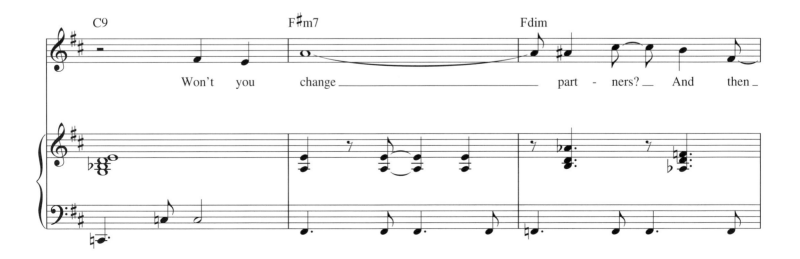

Won't you change _____ part - ners? __ And then _

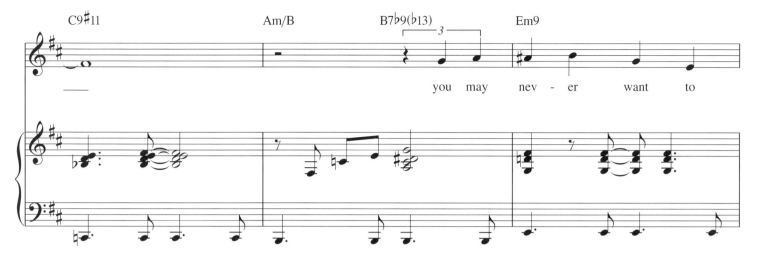

you may nev - er want to

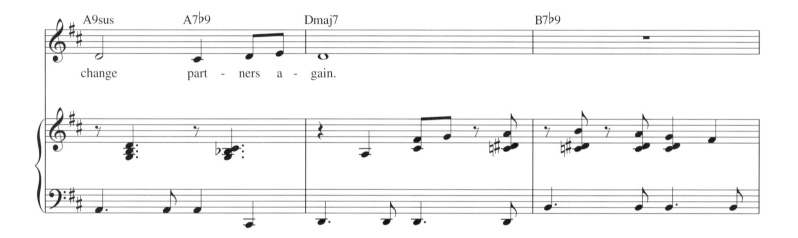

change part - ners a - gain.

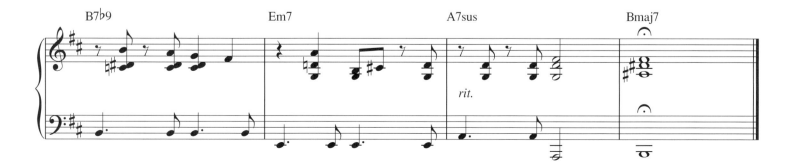

CHEEK TO CHEEK

from the RKO Radio Motion Picture TOP HAT

Words and Music by
IRVING BERLIN

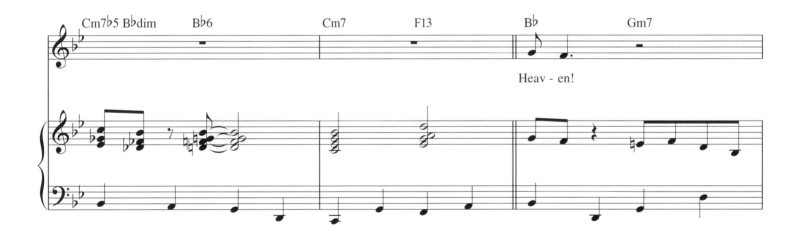

Heav - en!

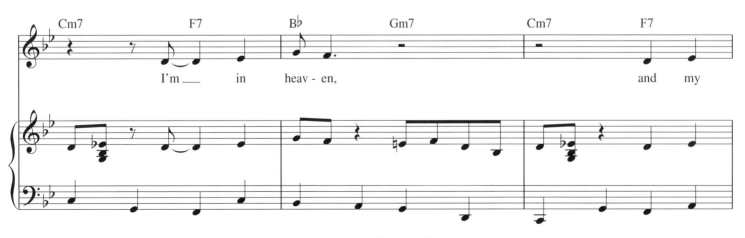

I'm ___ in heav - en, and my

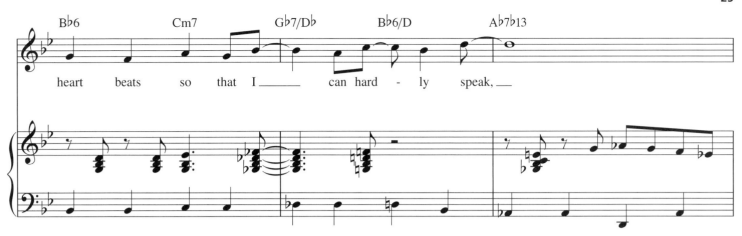

heart beats so that I _____ can hard - ly speak, ___

and I seem to find ___ the hap - pi - ness ___ I

seek when we're out to - geth - er, danc -

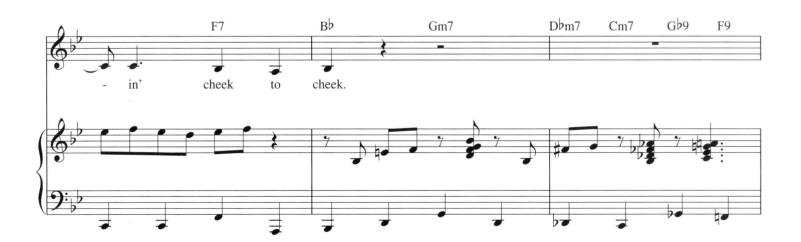

- in' cheek to cheek.

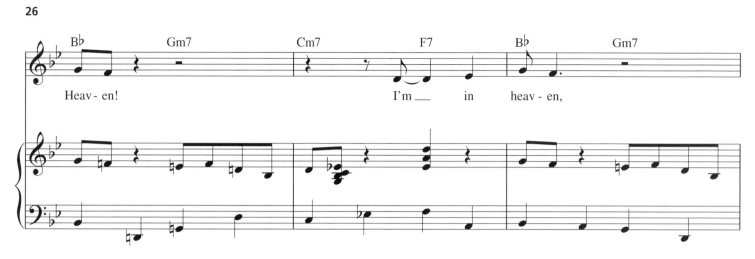

Heav - en! I'm ___ in heav - en,

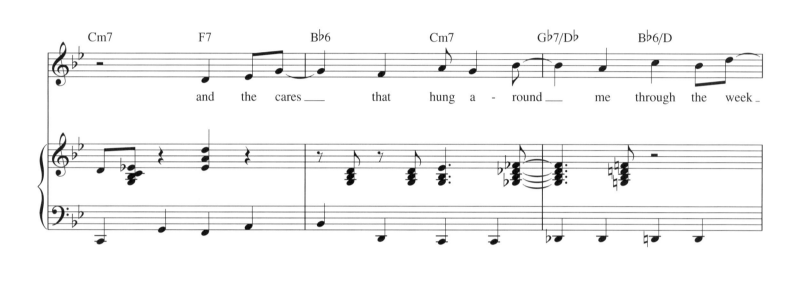

and the cares ___ that hung a - round ___ me through the week ___

___ seem to van - ish like ___ a gam -

- bler's luck - y streak, when we're

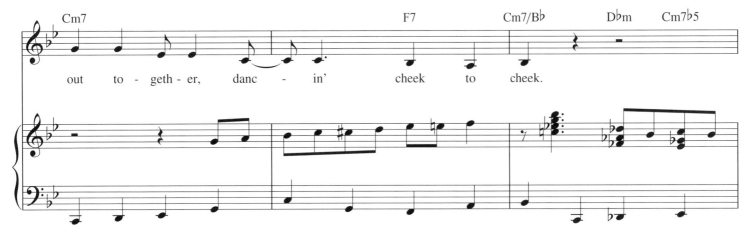

out to - geth - er, danc - in' cheek to cheek.

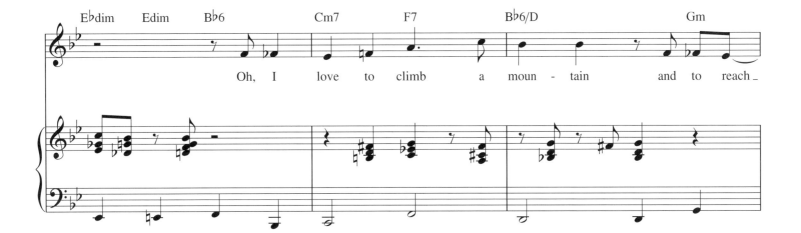

Oh, I love to climb a moun - tain and to reach ___

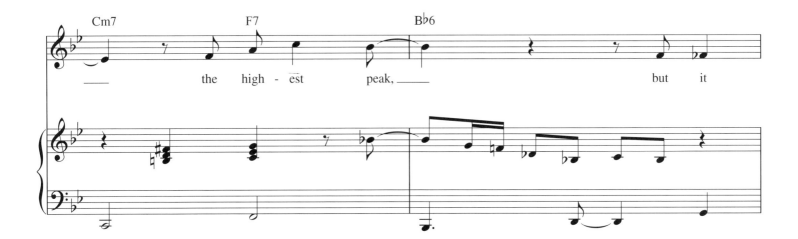

___ the high - est peak, ___ but it

does - n't thrill me half as much ___ as

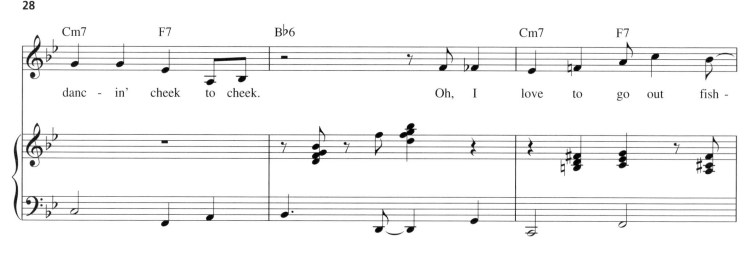

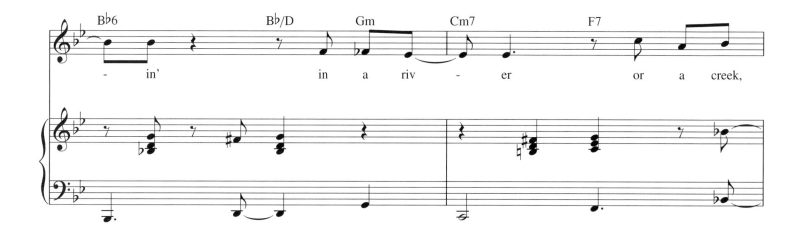

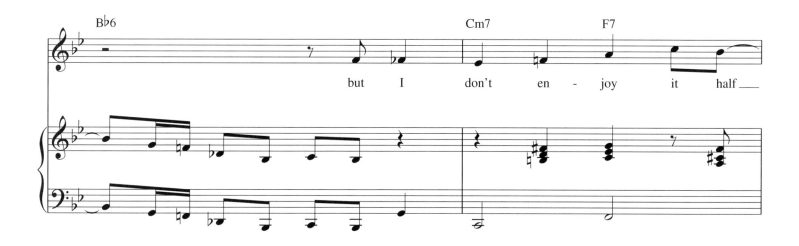

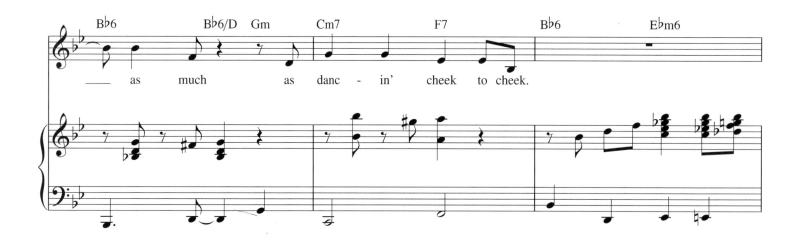

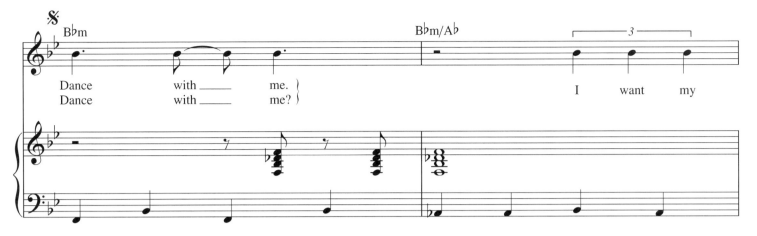

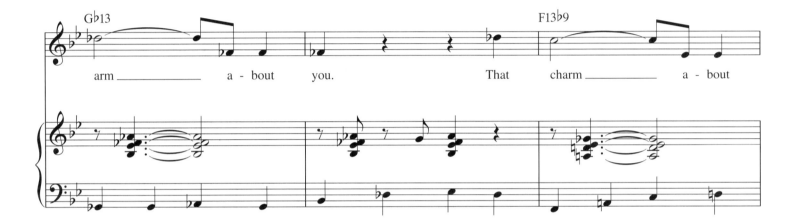

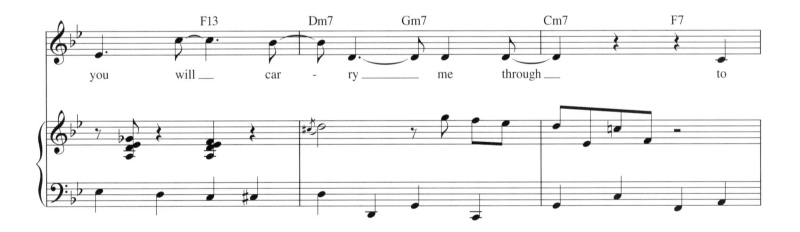

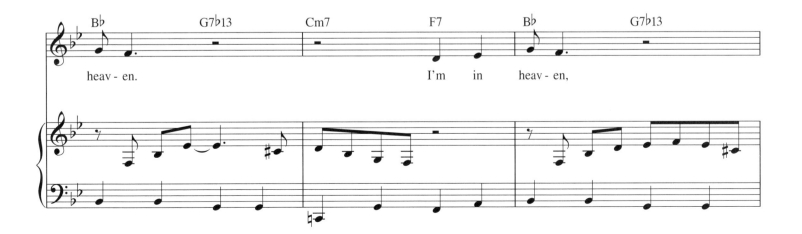

and my heart beats so that I _____ can hard - ly speak. _____

And I seem to find ___ that

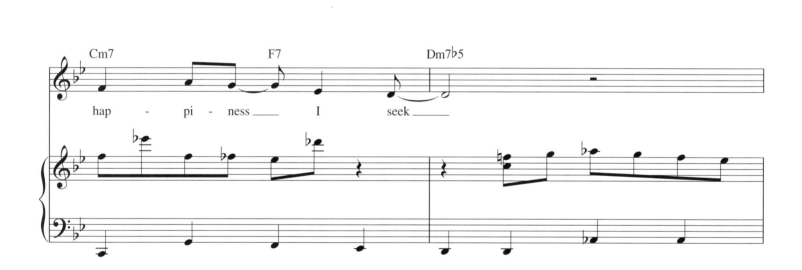

hap - pi - ness ___ I seek _____

To Coda ⊕

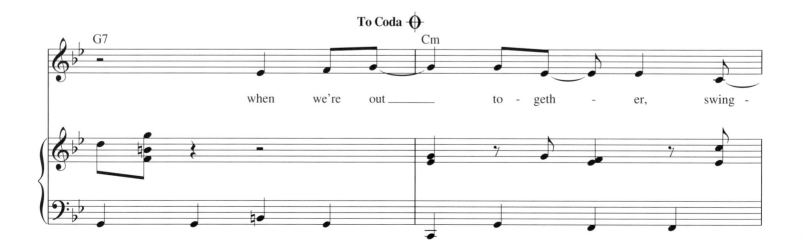

when we're out _____ to - geth - er, swing -

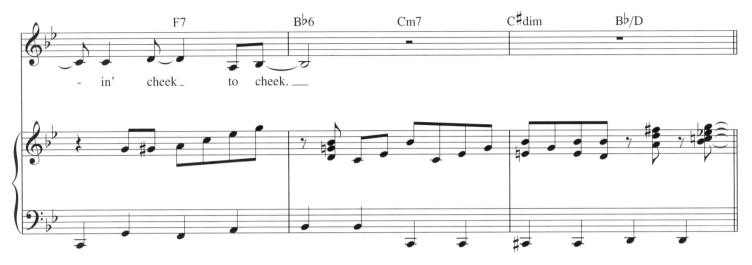

- in' cheek _ to cheek. _

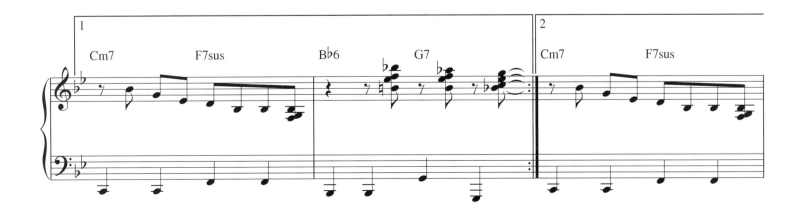

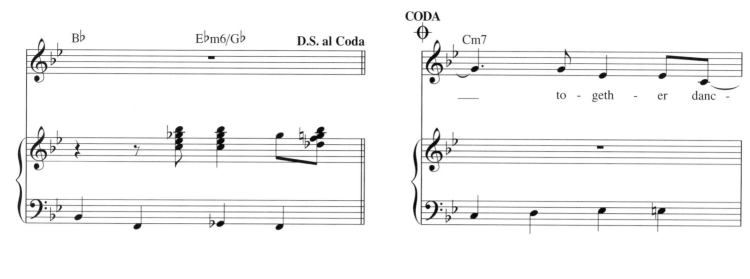

D.S. al Coda

CODA

to - geth - er danc -

- in', out to - geth - er danc - in',

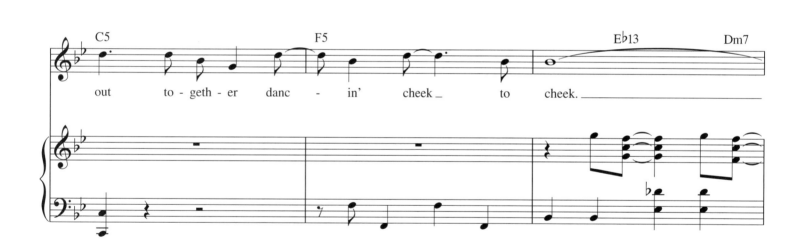

out to - geth - er danc - in' cheek _ to cheek. _____

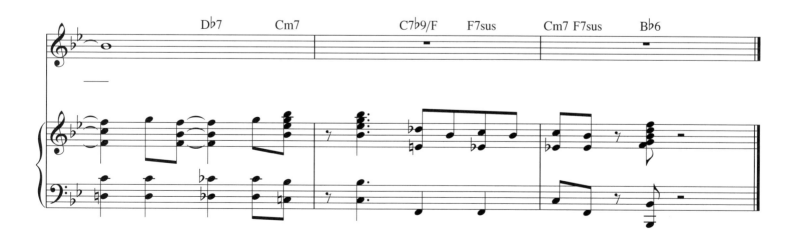

THE CONTINENTAL

Words by HERB MAGIDSON
Music by CON CONRAD

Moderate Swing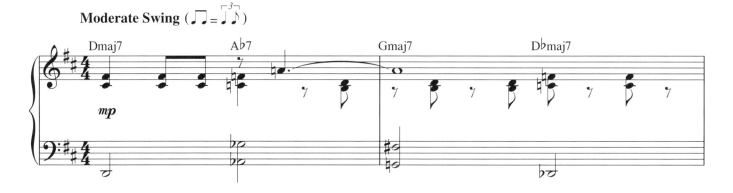

It's some - thing dar - ing, the Con - ti -
nen - tal, a way of danc - ing that's real - ly ul - tra
new. It's ver - y sub - tle, the Con - ti - nen - tal, be - cause it
does what you want it to do.

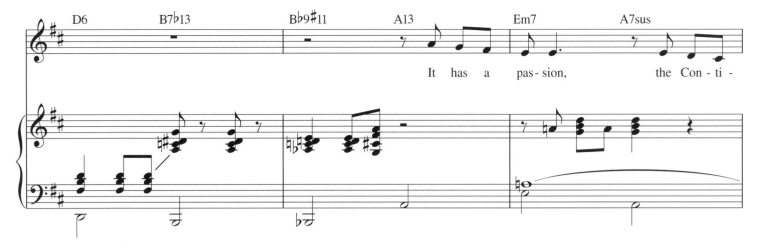

It has a pas-sion, the Con-ti-

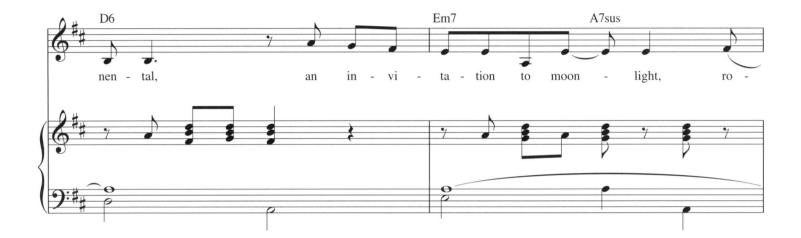

nen-tal, an in-vi-ta-tion to moon-light, ro-

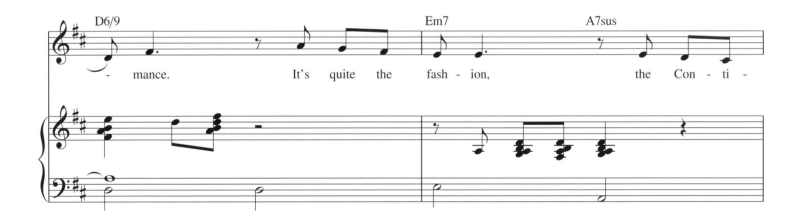

-mance. It's quite the fash-ion, the Con-ti-

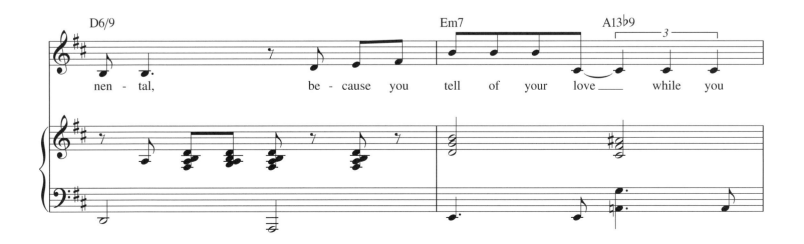

nen-tal, be-cause you tell of your love ___ while you

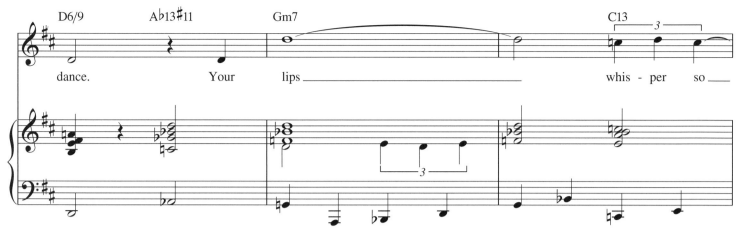

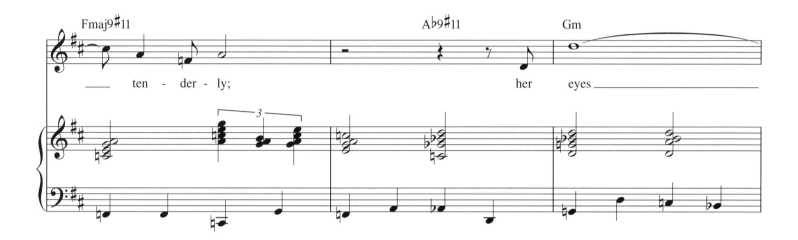

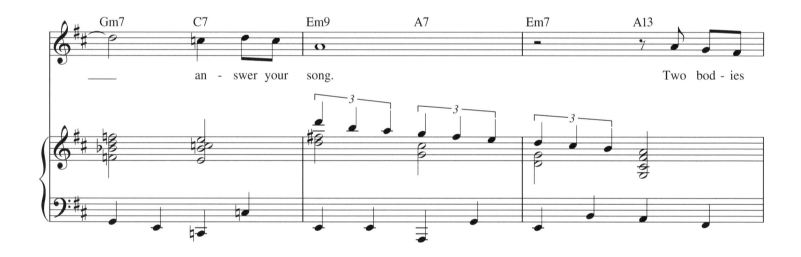

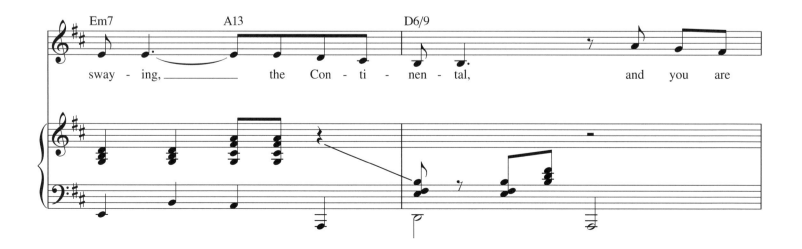

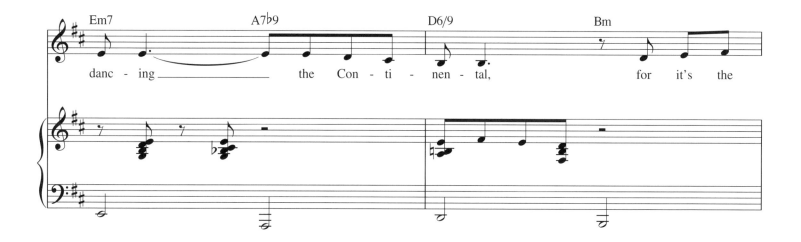

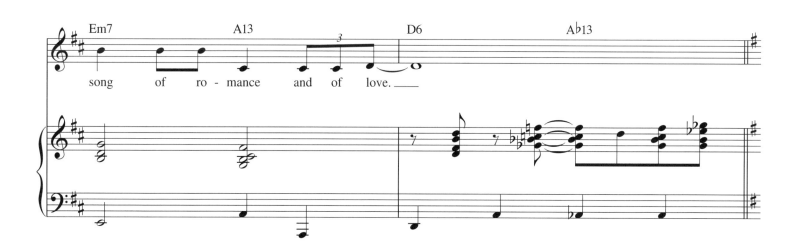

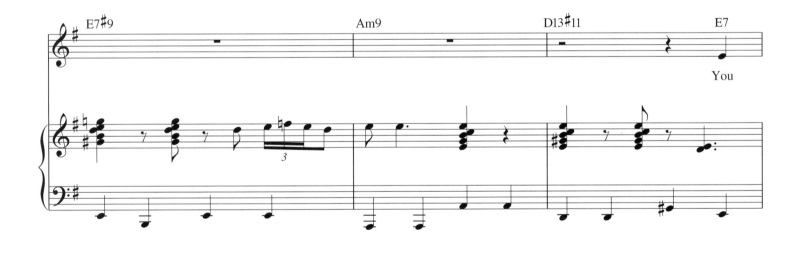

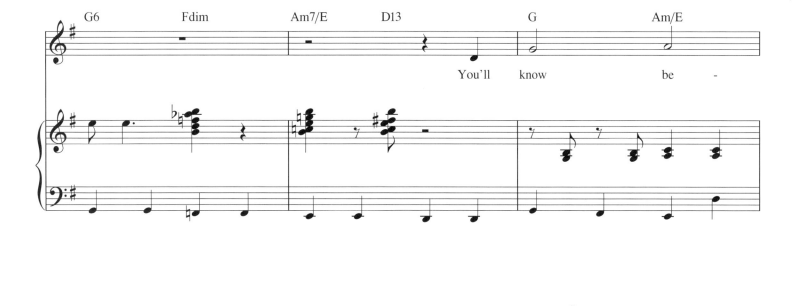

You'll know be -

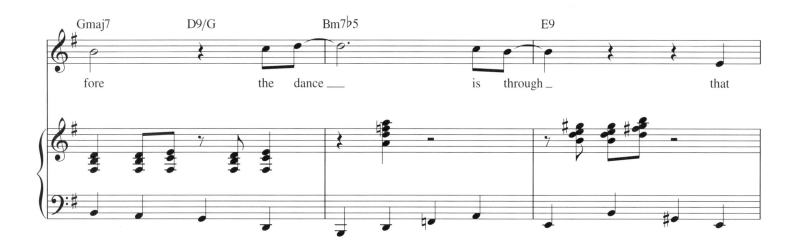

fore   the dance ___   is through ___   that

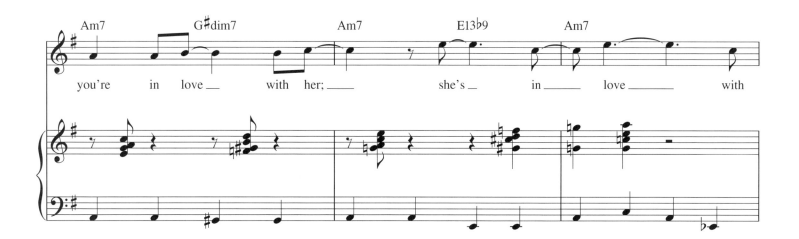

you're   in   love ___   with her; ___   she's ___   in ___ love ___   with

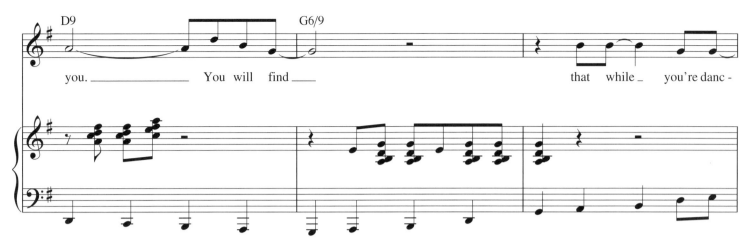

you. _____ You will find ___ that while _ you're danc -

- ing, there's a rhy - thm in your

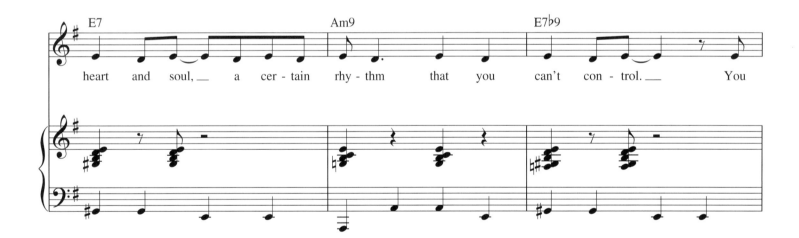

heart and soul, _ a cer - tain rhy - thm that you can't con - trol. ___ You

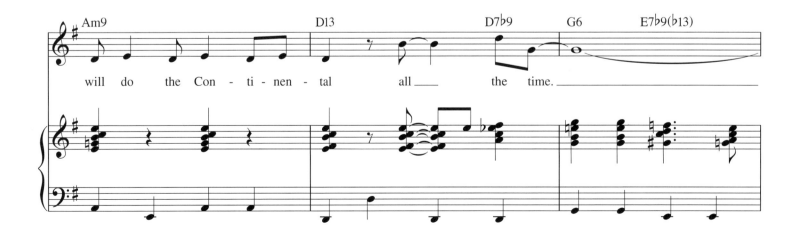

will do the Con - ti - nen - tal all ___ the time. _____

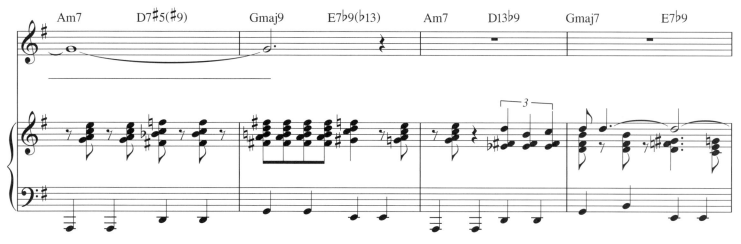

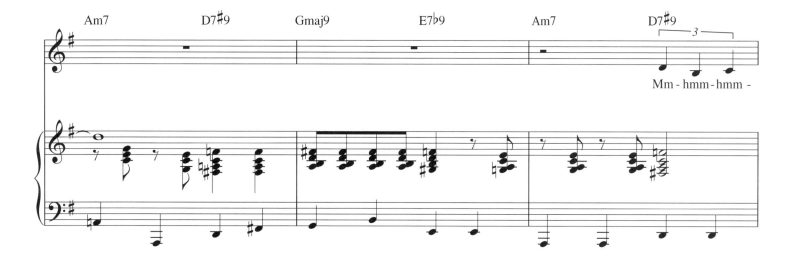

Mm - hmm - hmm -

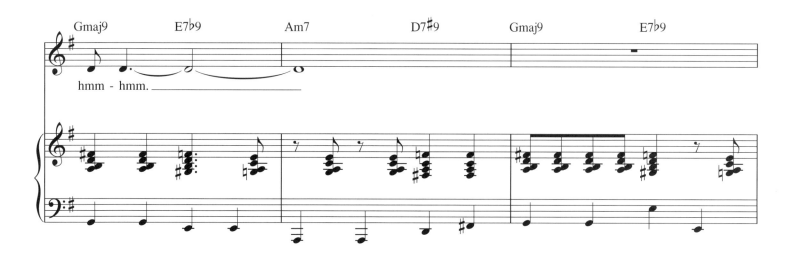

hmm - hmm.

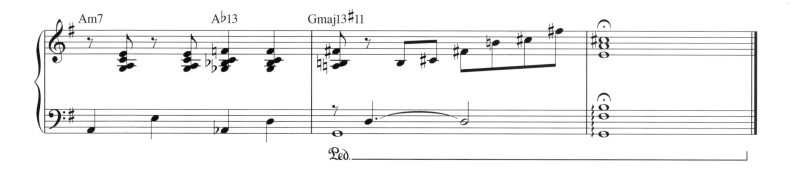

COME DANCE WITH ME

Words by SAMMY CAHN
Music by JAMES VAN HEUSEN

Moderately fast Swing

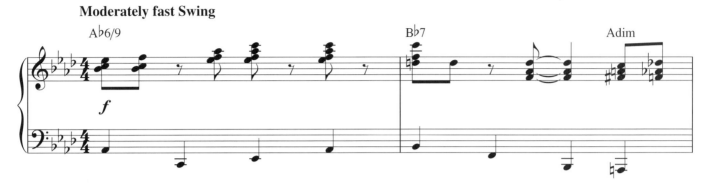

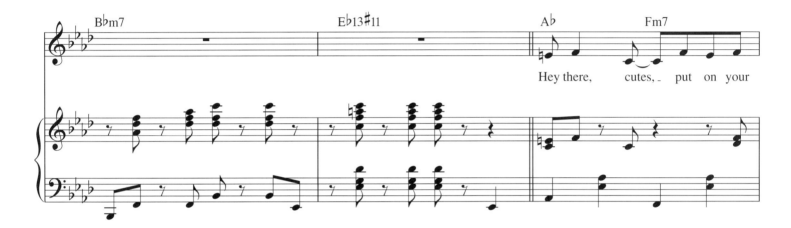

Hey there, cutes,_ put on your

danc - in' boots _ and come dance with me. _____

Come, _ dance with me. What an eve - nin'

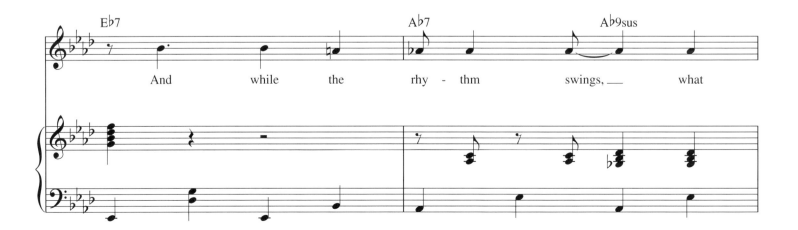

love - ly things _ I'll be ____ say - in',   'cause _

_ what is danc - in' but mak - in' love _ set to mu - sic

play - in'.   When the band _ be - gins to leave the stand _ and

folks start to roam, ___   as we waltz home _

_____ cheek to cheek, we'll be... _____

Come on, come on, come on, _____ come on and dance with me. _____

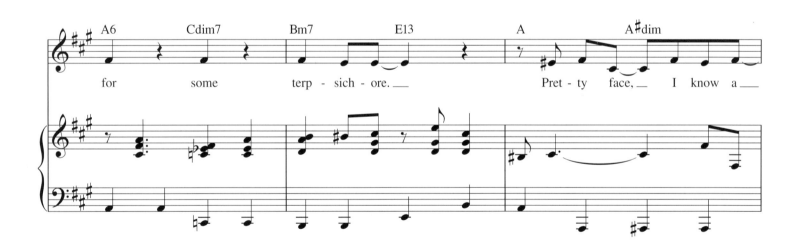

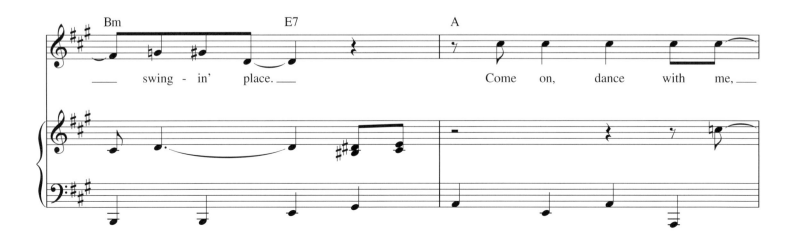

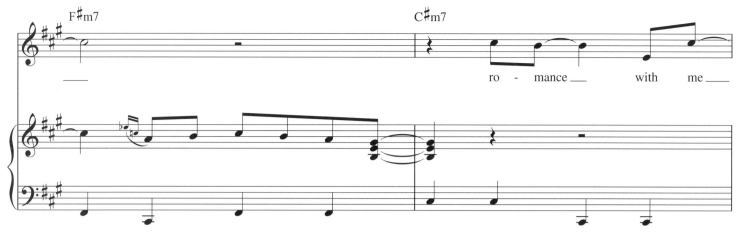

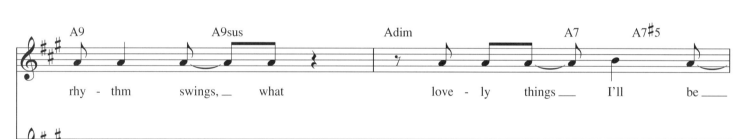

mak - in' love, ___ set to mu - sic

play - in'? ___ When the band ___ be - gins to

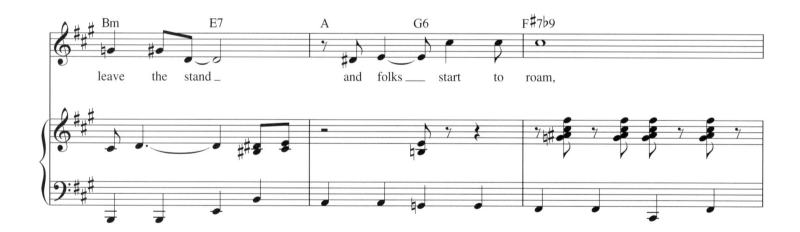

leave the stand ___ and folks ___ start to roam,

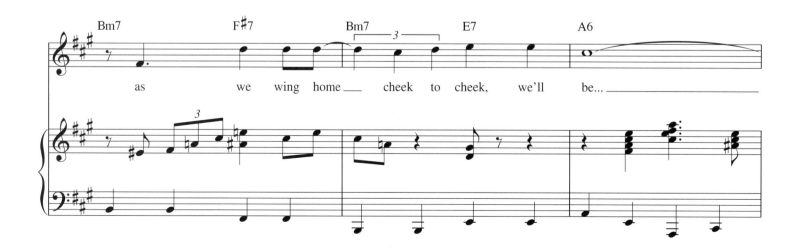

as we wing home ___ cheek to cheek, we'll be... ___

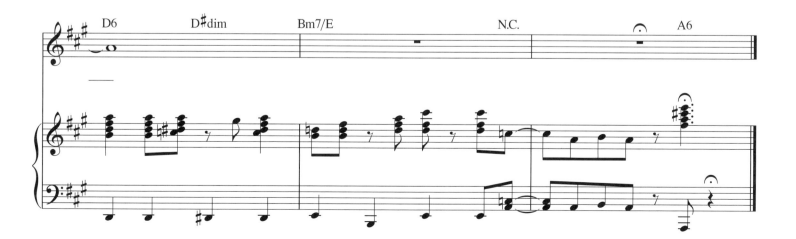

THE DAYS OF WINE AND ROSES

Lyric by JOHNNY MERCER
Music by HENRY MANCINI

Moderate Swing

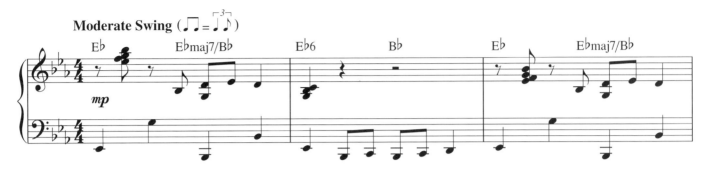

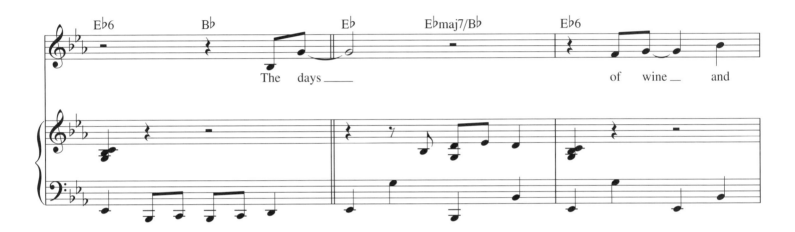

The days ____ of wine __ and

ros - es ____ laugh and run a - way, ____

like a child ____ at play, ____ through ____ the

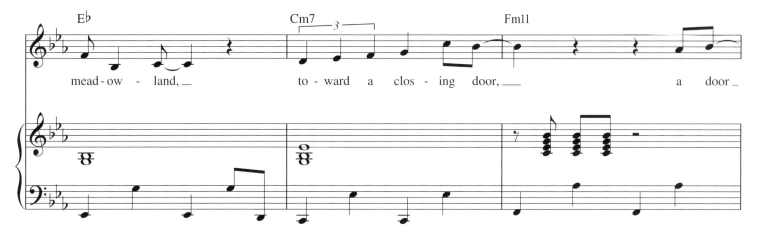

meadow - land, __ toward a clos - ing door, __ a door __

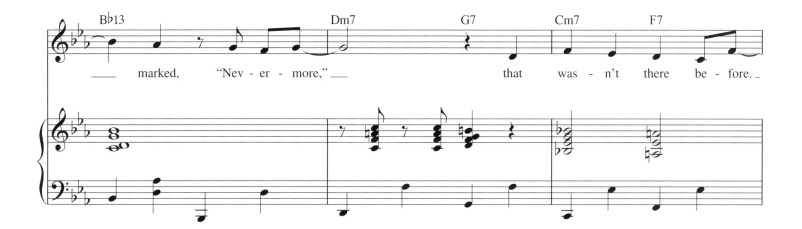

__ marked, "Nev - er - more," __ that was - n't there be - fore. __

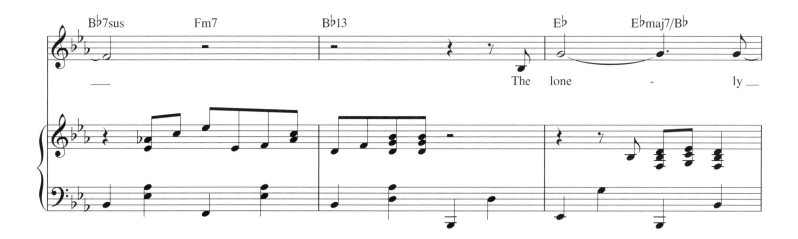

__ The lone - ly __

__ night dis - clos - es __ just a pass -

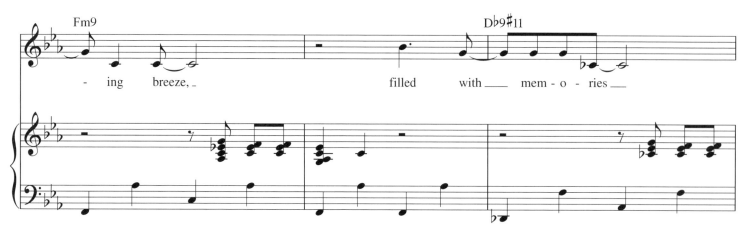

-ing breeze, filled with mem-o-ries

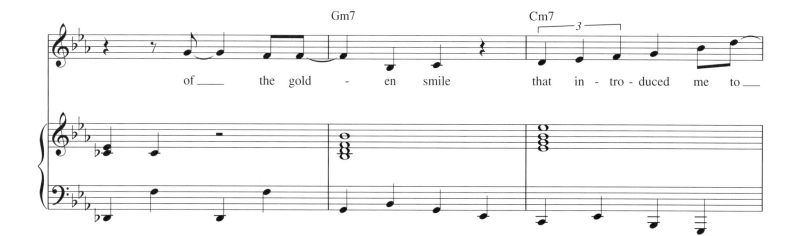

of the gold-en smile that in-tro-duced me to

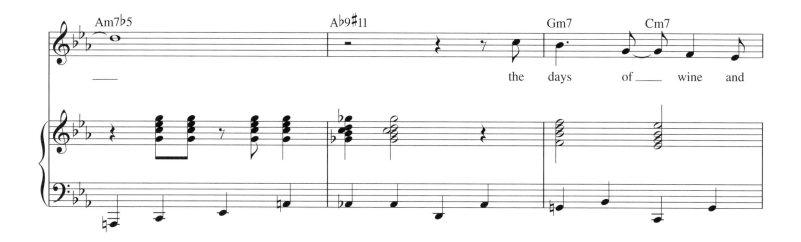

the days of wine and

ros - es and you.

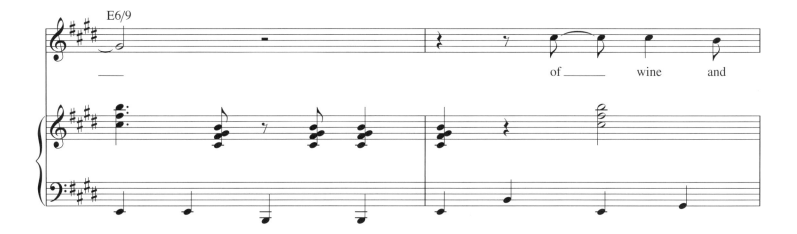

54

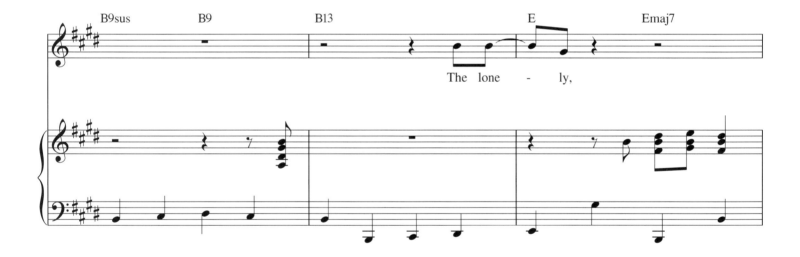

The lone - ly,

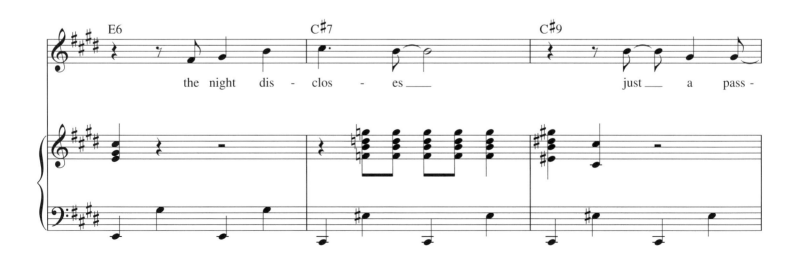

the night dis - clos - es _____ just _____ a pass -

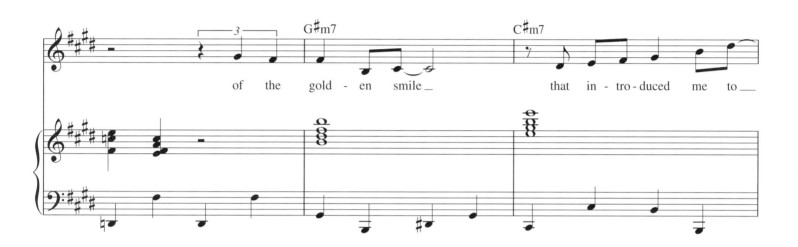

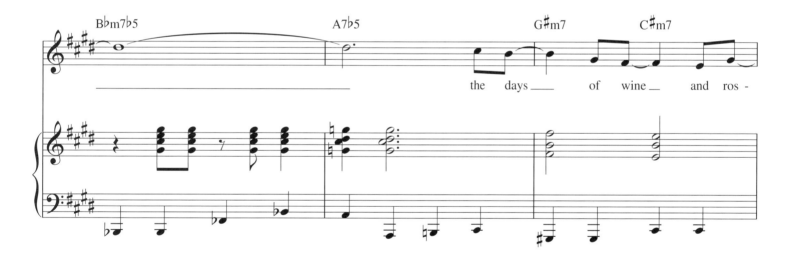

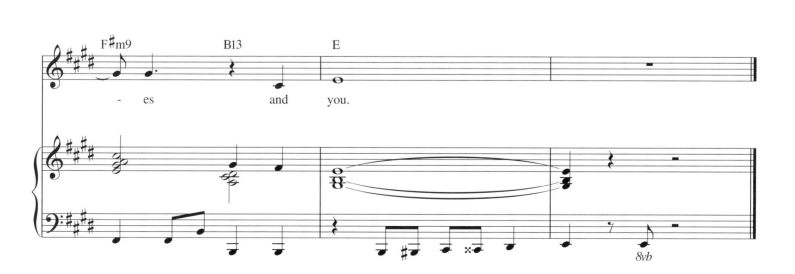

DON'T WORRY 'BOUT ME

Lyric by TED KOEHLER
Music by RUBE BLOOM

love. Let's say that our

lit - tle show is o - ver, and so the sto - ry ends.

Why not call it a day the sen - si - ble way,

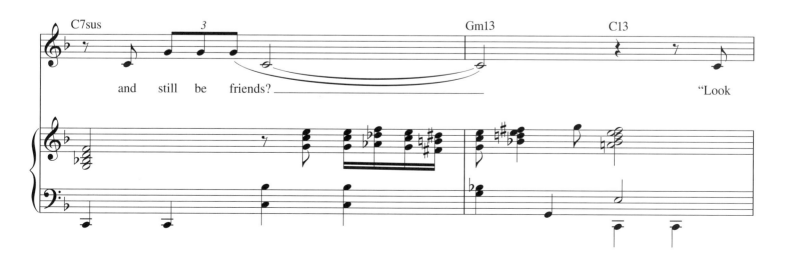

and still be friends? _____ "Look

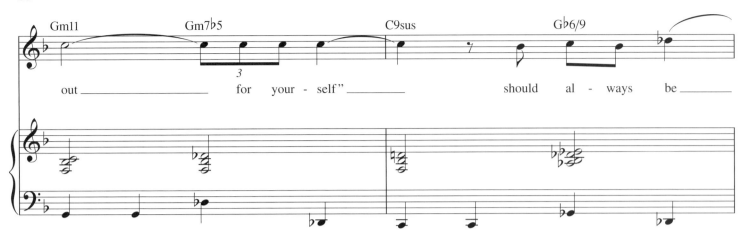

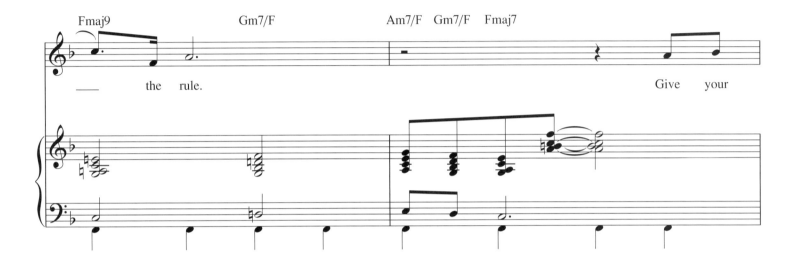

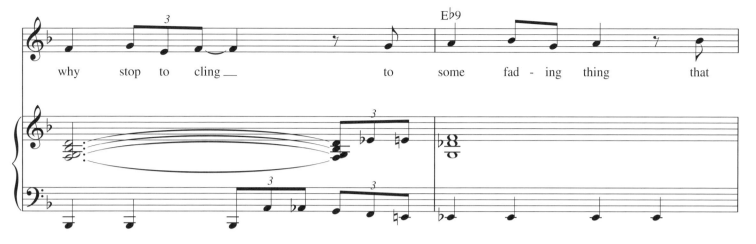

why stop to cling ___ to some fad - ing thing that

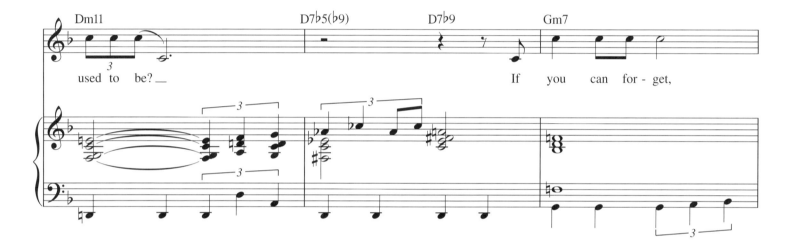

used to be? ___ If you can for - get,

don't you wor - ry 'bout ___ me. ___

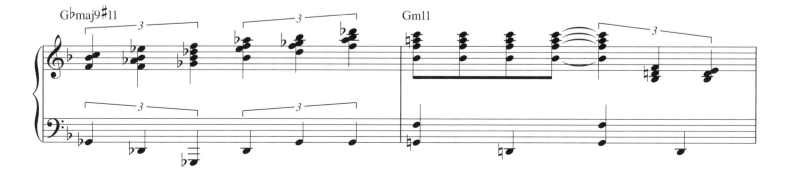

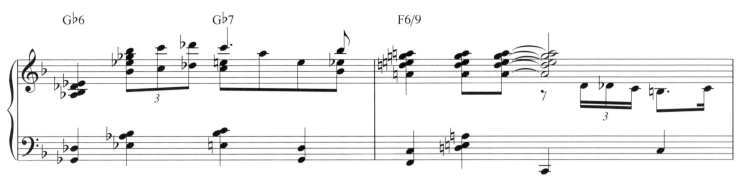

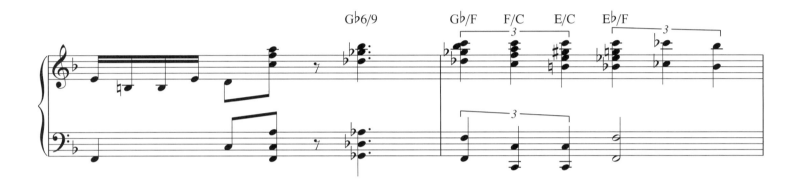

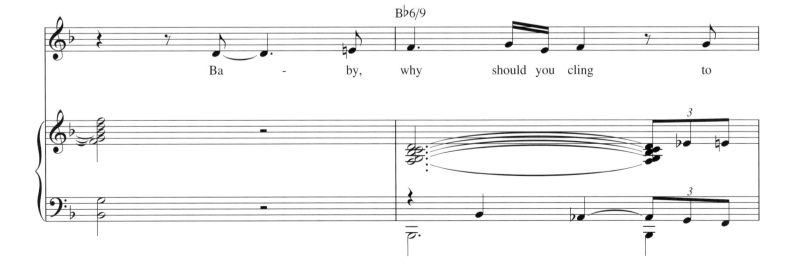

Ba - by, why should you cling to

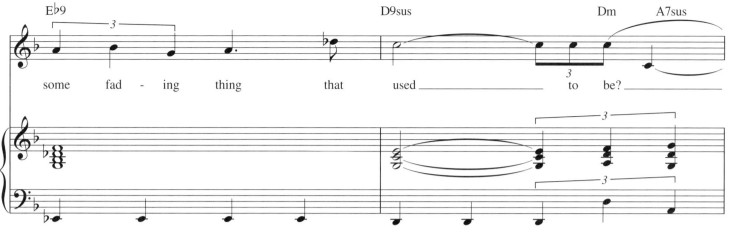

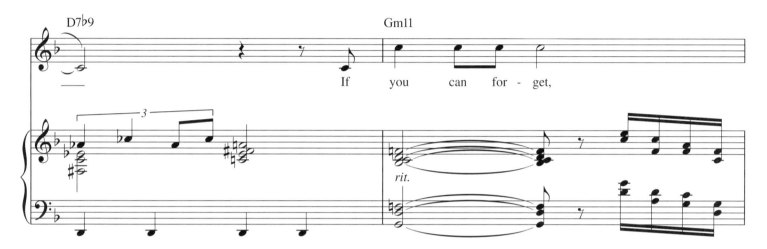

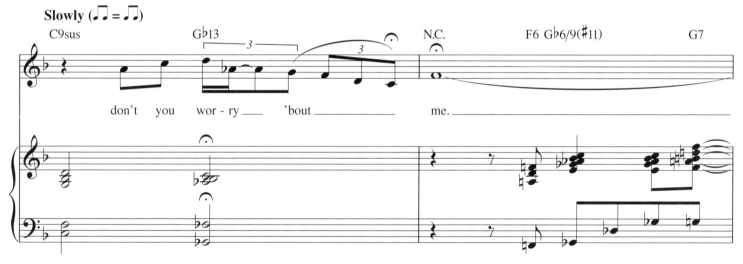

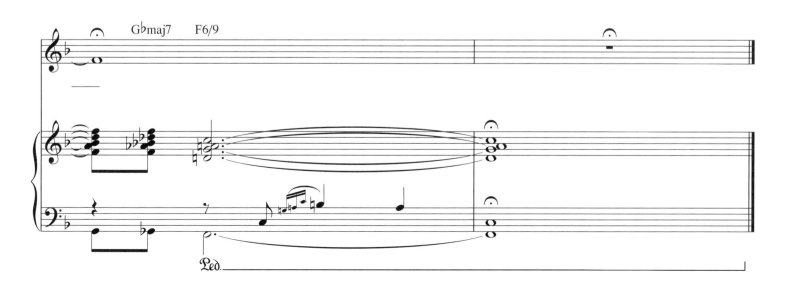

DON'CHA GO 'WAY MAD

Words and Music by AL STILLMAN
JIMMY MUNDY and ILLINOIS JACQUET

Who'd ev-er dream _ your cous-in would wan-der in-to that res-tau -

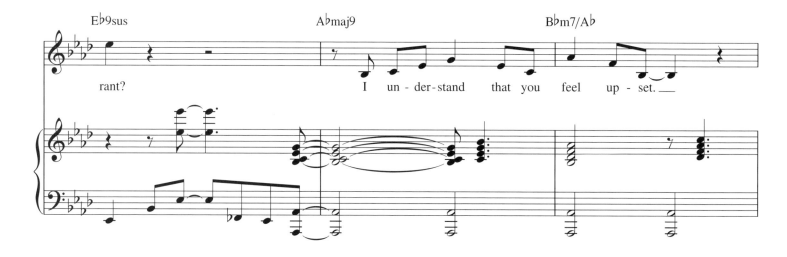

rant? I un-der-stand that you feel up-set. _

What do you say that you for-give and for-get? Come on and kiss me just to

show you're glad. _ Ba - by, ba - by, don'-cha go _ 'way mad. _

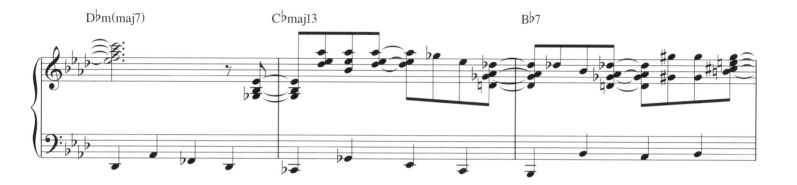

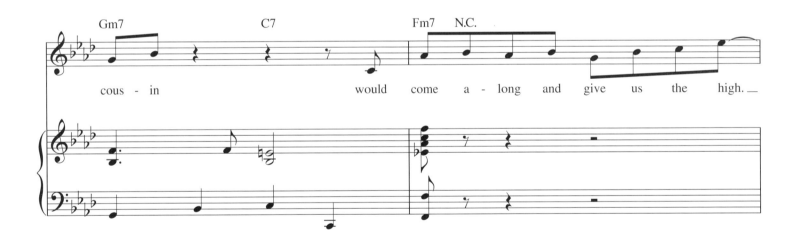

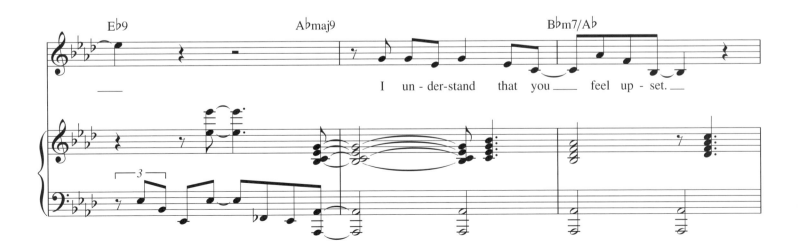

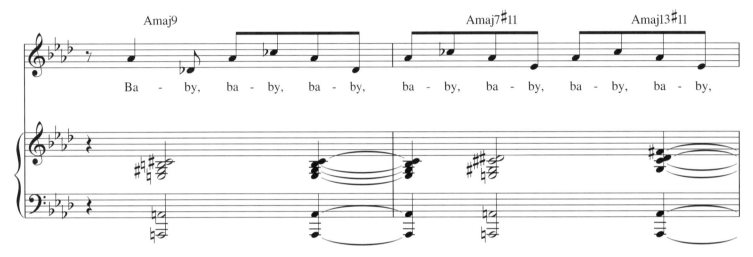

THE END OF A LOVE AFFAIR

Words and Music by
EDWARD C. REDDING

Moderate Ballad

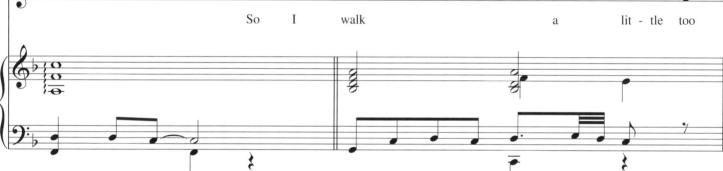

So I walk a lit-tle too

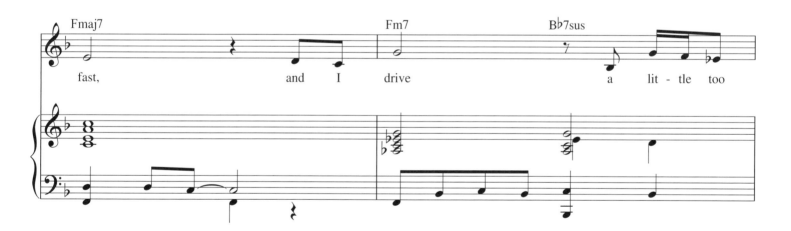

fast, and I drive a lit-tle too

fast, and I'm reck-less. It's true, __ but what else can you do

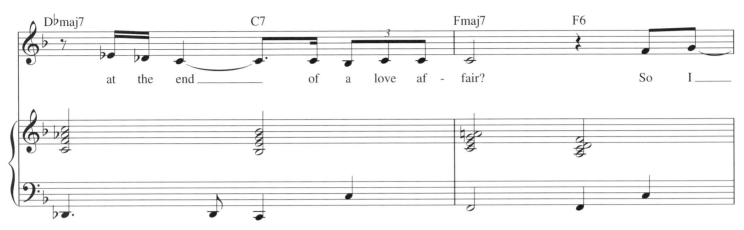

at the end _____ of a love af - fair? So I _____

_____ talk _____ a lit - tle too much, and I laugh a lit - tle

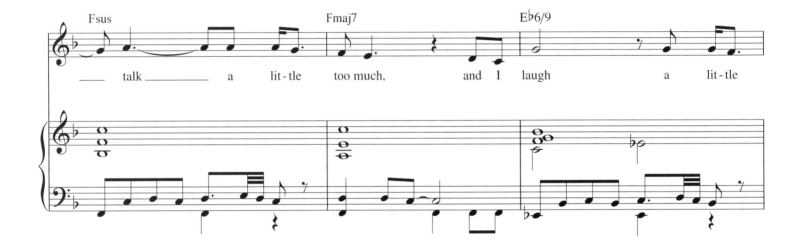

too much, and my voice is too loud when I'm

out in a crowd, so that peo - ple are apt to

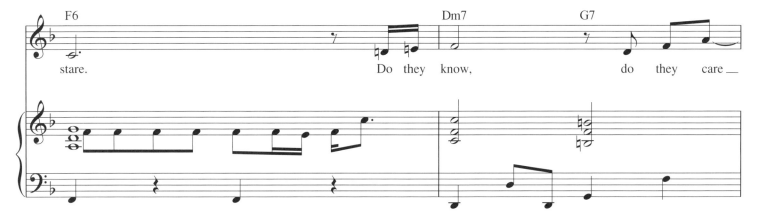

stare.   Do they know,   do they care __

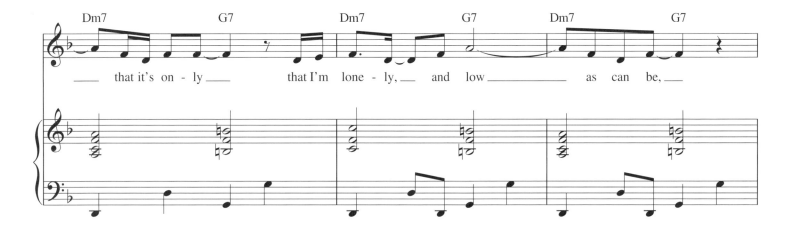

__ that it's on - ly ___   that I'm lone - ly, __ and low _____ as can be, __

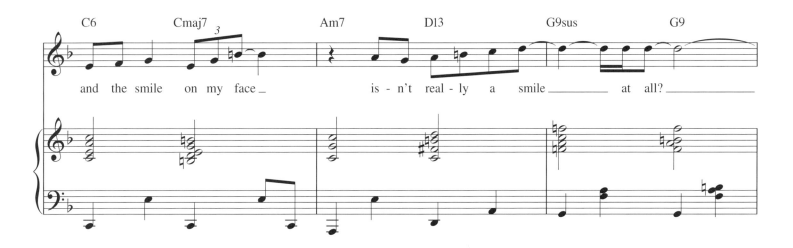

and the smile   on my face _   is - n't real - ly   a   smile _____ at all? _____

So   I smoke   a   lit - tle   too much,   and   I

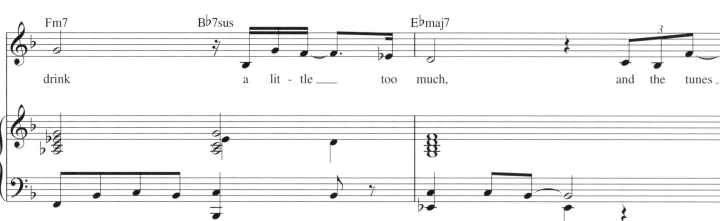

drink a lit - tle ___ too much, and the tunes ___

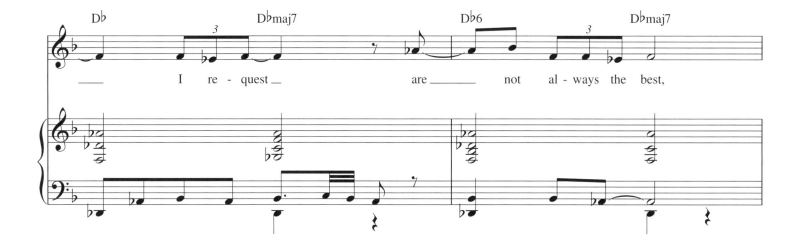

___ I re - quest ___ are ___ not al - ways the best,

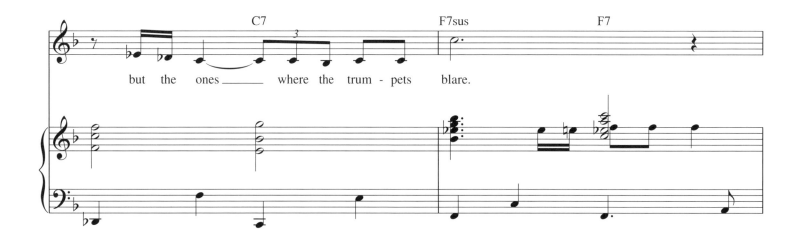

but the ones ___ where the trum - pets blare.

So I go ___ at a mad - d'ning pace, and

I pre-tend that it's tak - ing her place, but what else can you do

at the end __ of a __ love af - fair? _____

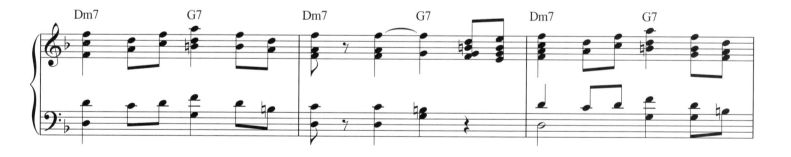

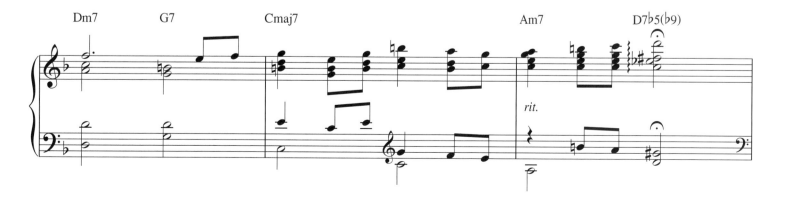

Tempo I

So I smoke __ a lit-tle

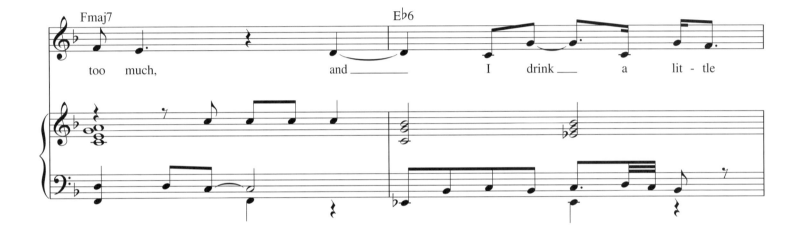

too much, and _____ I drink ___ a lit - tle

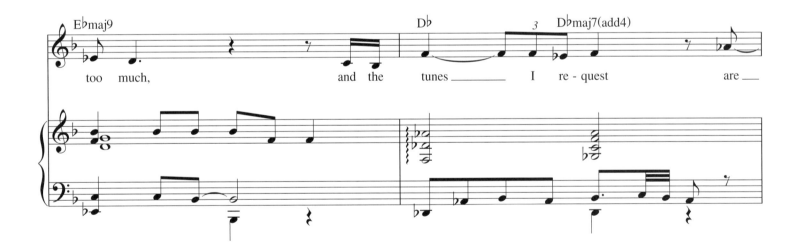

too much, and the tunes _____ I re - quest are ___

___ not al - ways the best, but the ones ___ where the trum - pets

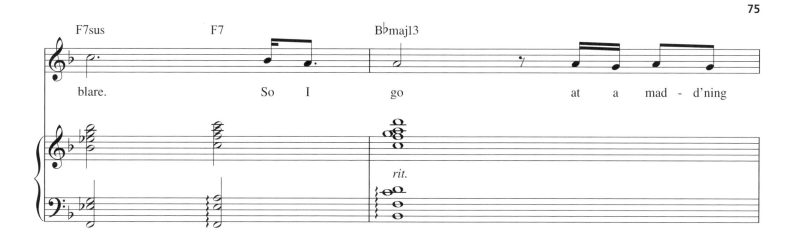

blare. So I go at a mad - d'ning

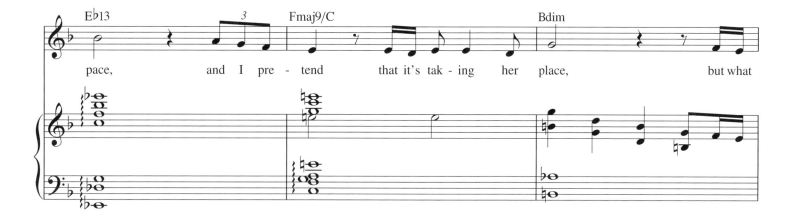

pace, and I pre - tend that it's tak - ing her place, but what

Tempo I

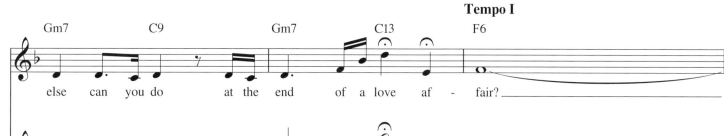

else can you do at the end of a love af - fair?_____

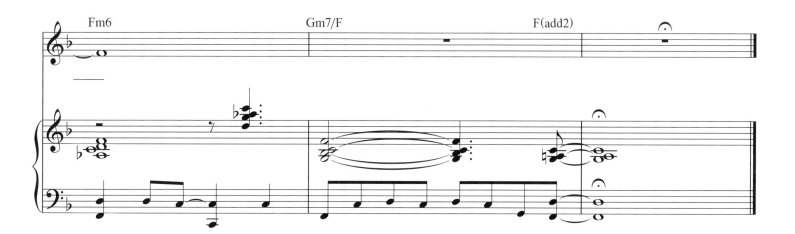

FLY ME TO THE MOON
(In Other Words)

Words and Music by
BART HOWARD

In oth-er words, _ ba - by, kiss

_ me. Fill my heart with song _ and let me sing _

_ for - ev-er-more. _ You _ are _ all I long _ for, all I

wor-ship and a - dore. _ In oth er words, _ please be true. _

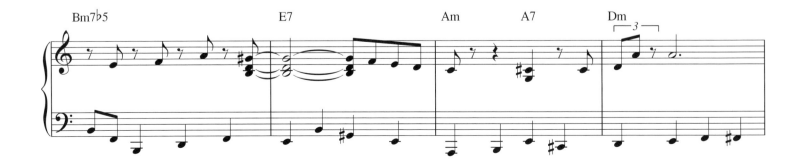

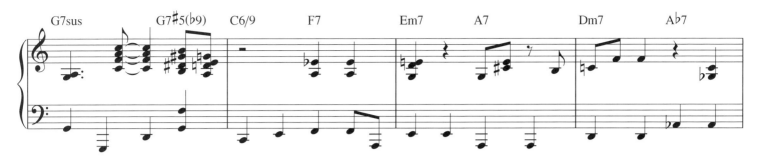

Fill my heart with song

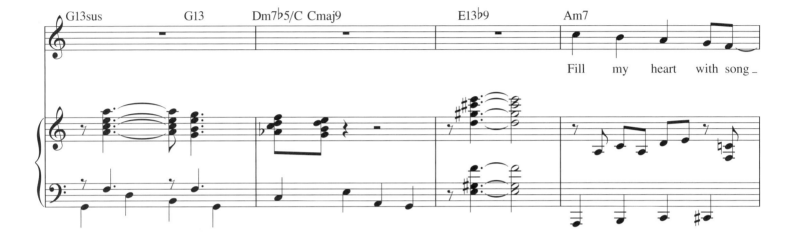

__ and let me sing __ for - ev - er - more. __ You _

__ are _ all I long _ for, all I wor-ship and a - dore. _

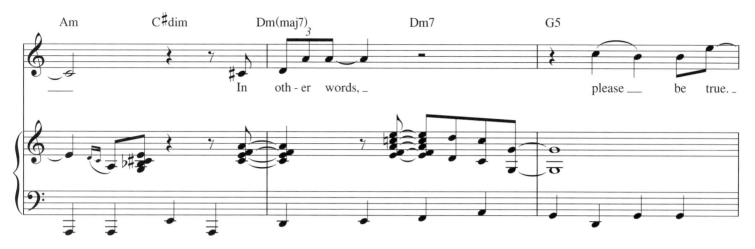

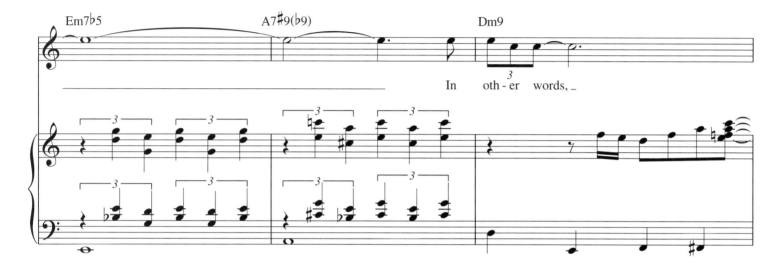

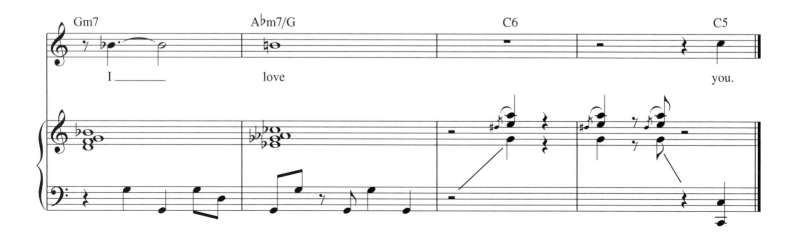

THE GOOD LIFE

Words by JACK REARDON
and JEAN BROUSSOLLE
Music by SACHA DISTEL

It's the good life, full of fun, ___ seems to be the i-

deal. Yes, the good life lets you hide ___

___ all the sad-ness you feel. ___ You won't

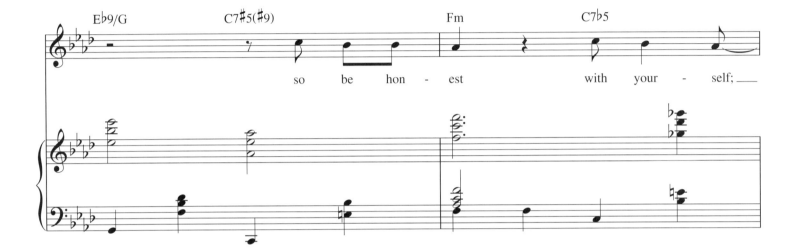

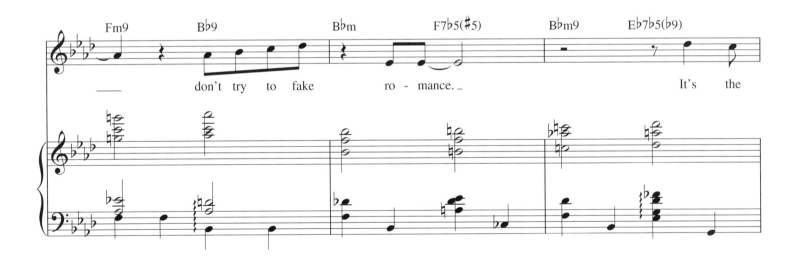

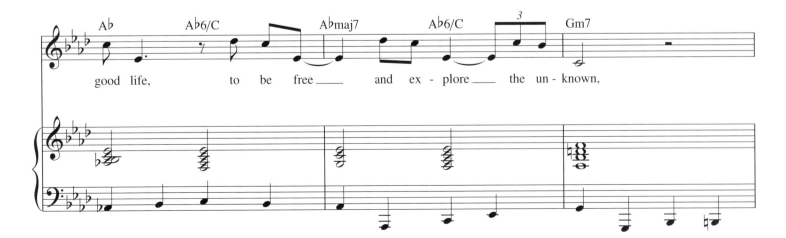

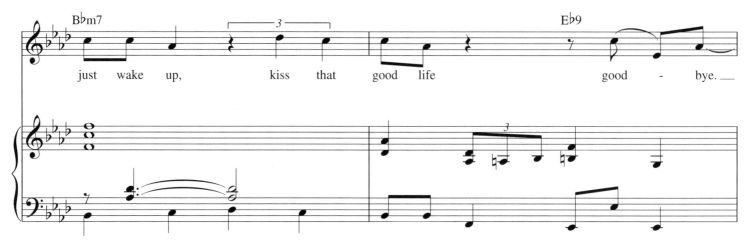

Bbm7   Eb9

just wake up,   kiss that good life   good - bye. __

Ab   Eb7sus   Ab   Eb7#9   Abmaj7

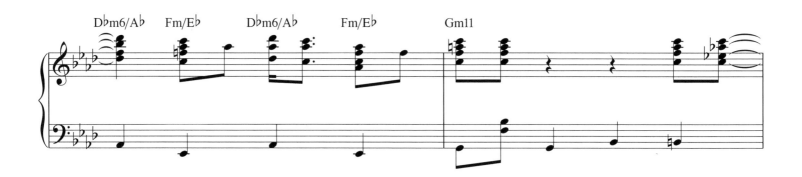

Dbm6/Ab   Fm/Eb   Dbm6/Ab   Fm/Eb   Gm11

C7#5(#9)   Fm6   Fm7

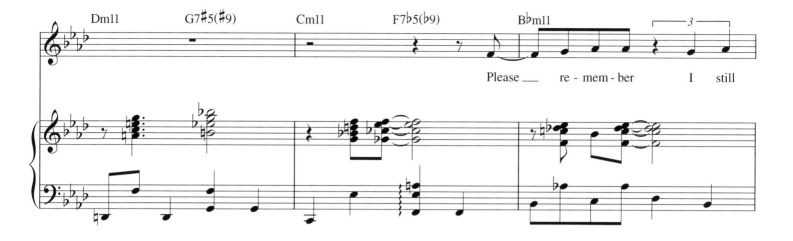

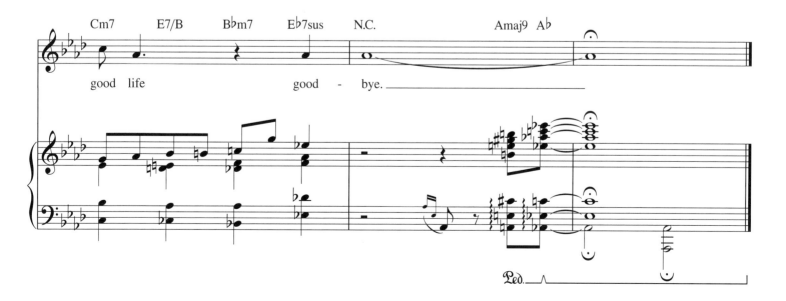

HOW LITTLE WE KNOW

Words by CAROLYN LEIGH
Music by PHILIP SPRINGER

How lit-tle we know, how much to dis-

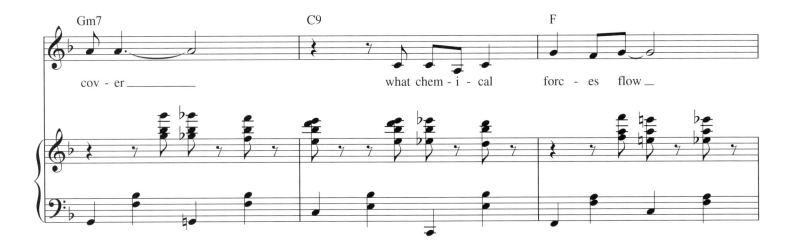

cov-er _____ what chem-i-cal forc-es flow __

from lov-er to lov-er. _____ How lit-tle we

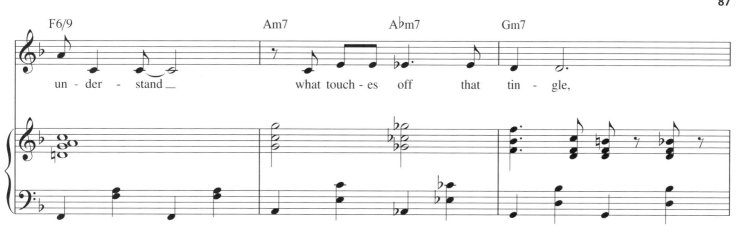

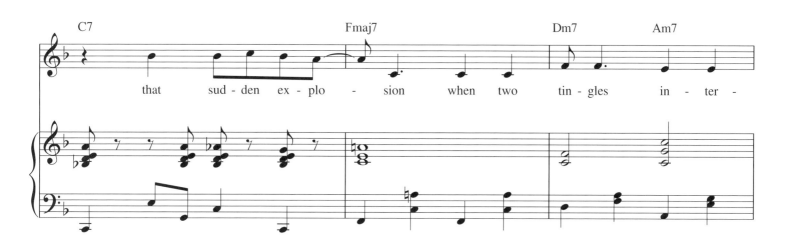

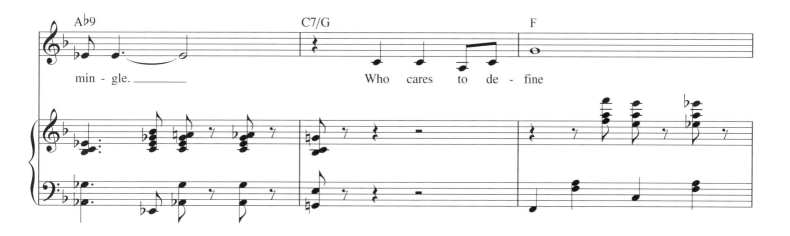

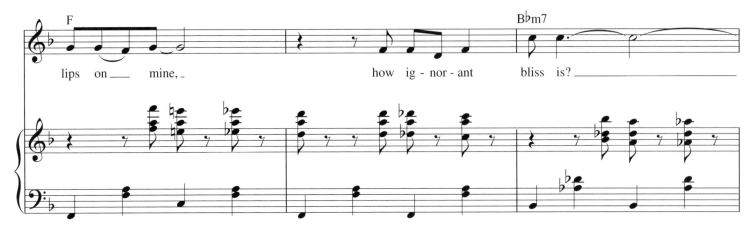

lips on __ mine, __ how ig - nor - ant bliss is? _____

__ So long as you kiss me and the world a - round us

shat - ters, _____ how lit - tle it mat - ters

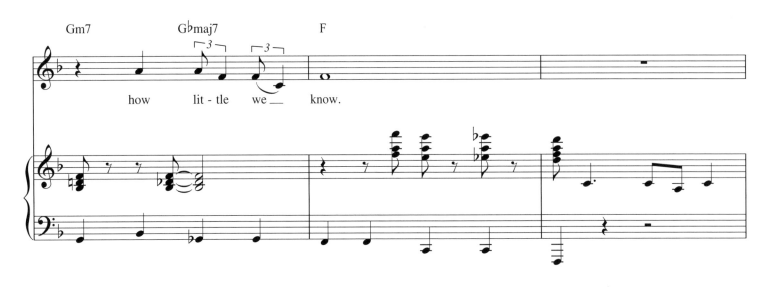

how lit - tle we __ know.

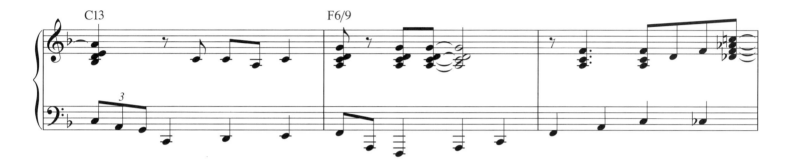

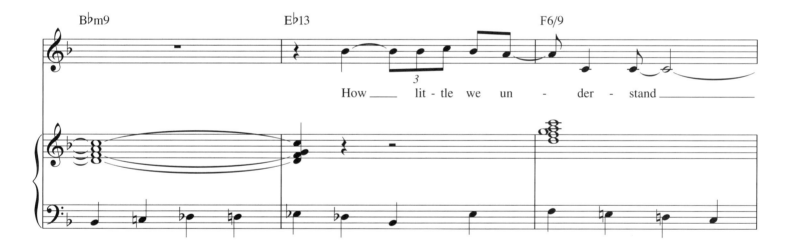

How ____ lit - tle we un - der - stand _____

____ what touch - es off that tin - gle, ____ that sud - den ex - plo -

-sion when two tin - gles _____ in - ter - min - gle.

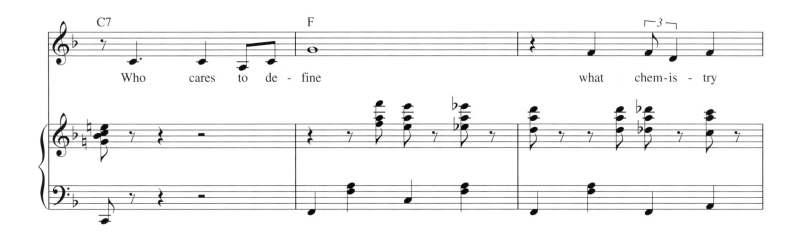

Who cares to de - fine what chem-is - try

this is? _____ Who cares, _ with your lips on _ mine,

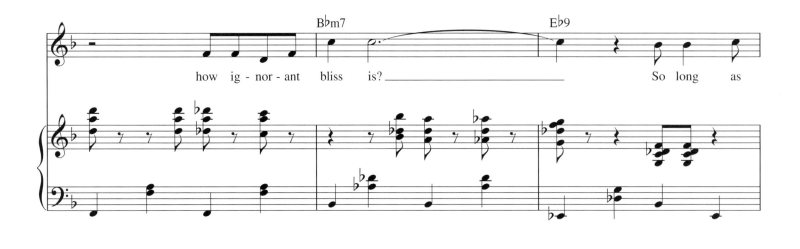

how ig - nor - ant bliss is? _____ So long as

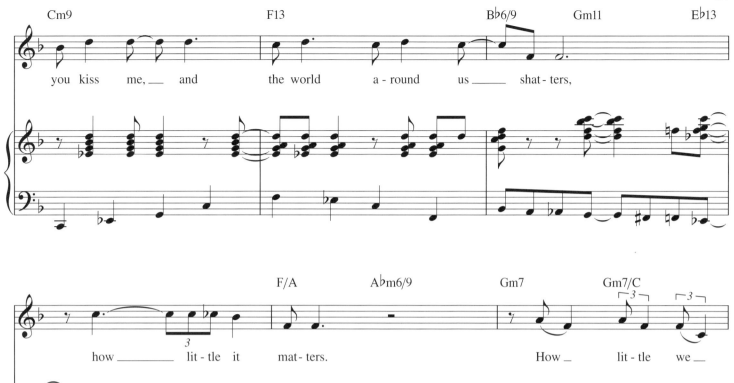

you kiss me, __ and the world a - round us __ shat - ters,

how __ lit - tle it mat - ters. How __ lit - tle we __

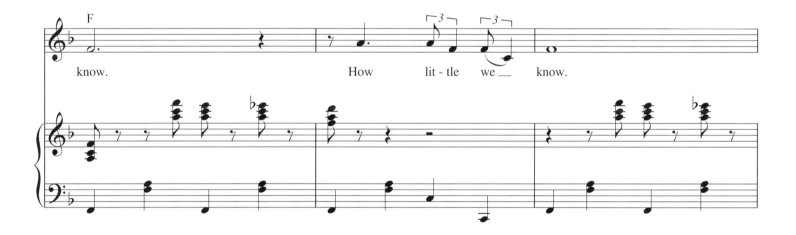

know. How lit - tle we __ know.

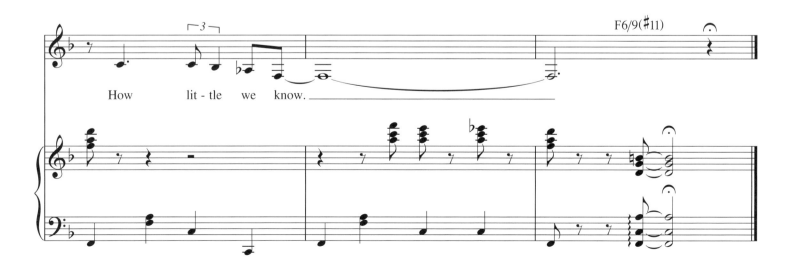

How lit - tle we know. _____

I CONCENTRATE ON YOU

Words and Music by
COLE PORTER

Moderate Bossa

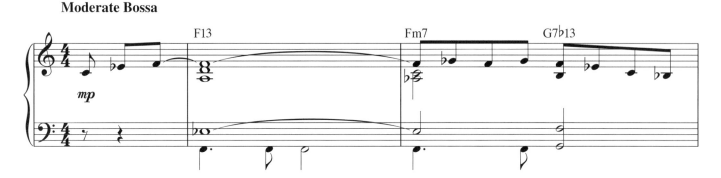

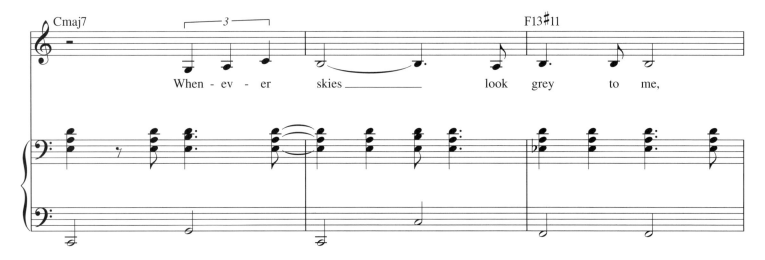

When - ev - er skies _____ look grey to me,

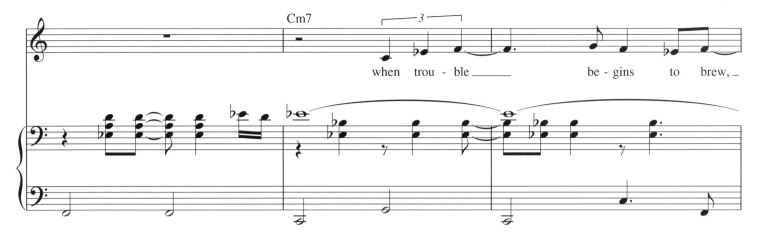

when trou - ble _____ be - gins to brew, _

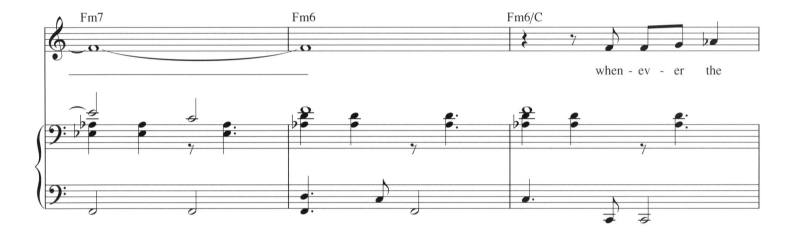

when - ev - er the

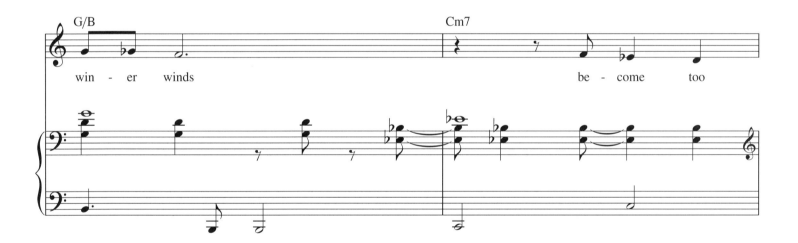

win - er winds be - come too

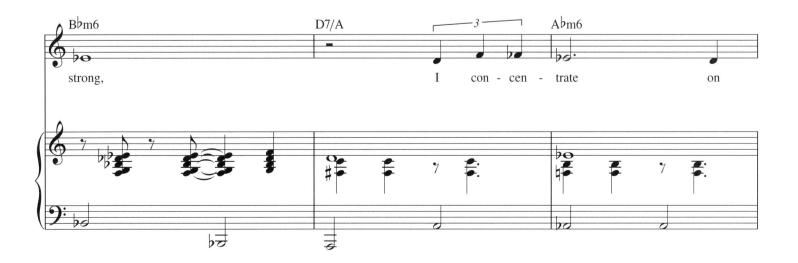

strong, I con - cen - trate on

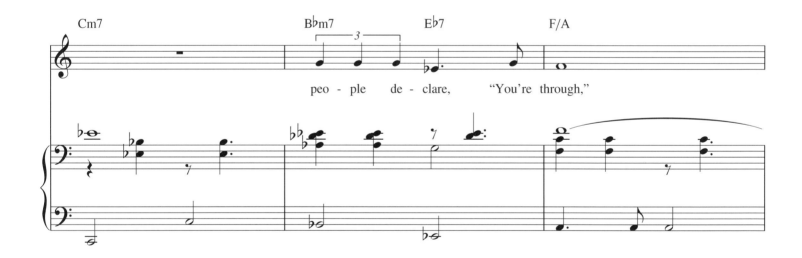

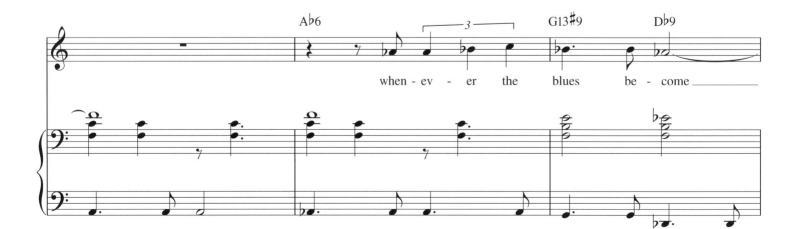

my on - ly song, con - cen -

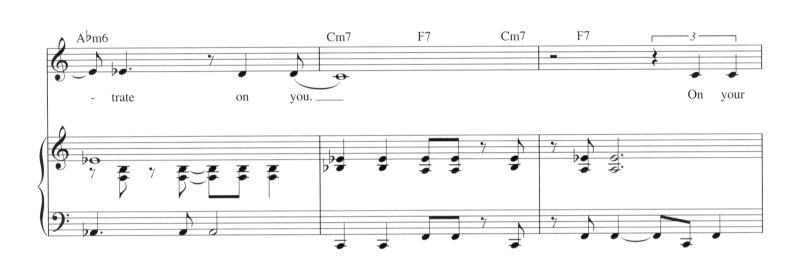

- trate on you. ____ On your

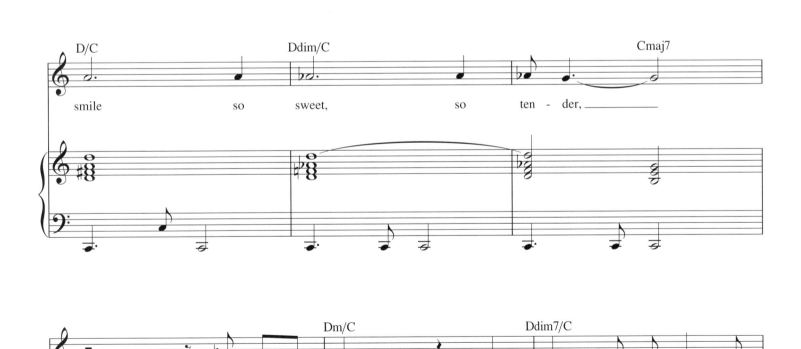

smile so sweet, so ten - der, _____

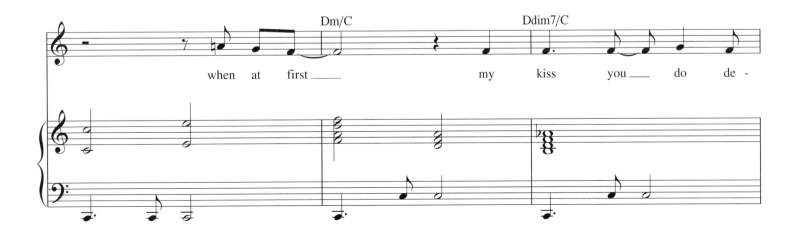

when at first ____ my kiss you ____ do de -

cline; on the light in your

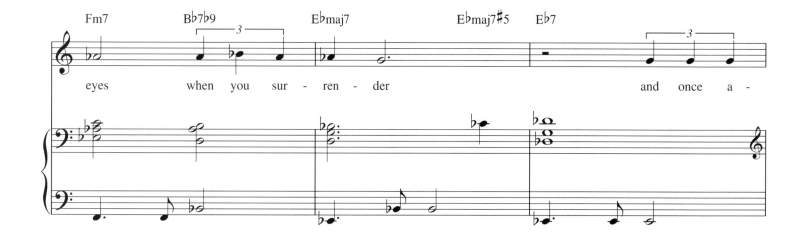

eyes when you sur - ren - der and once a -

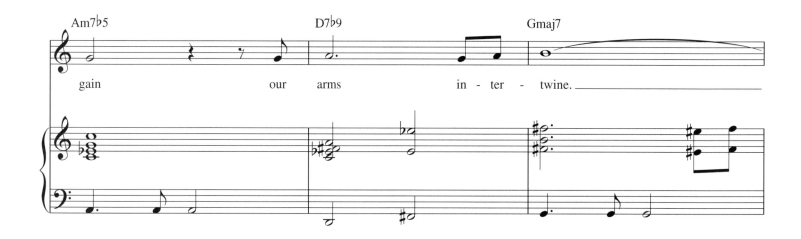

gain our arms in - ter - twine.

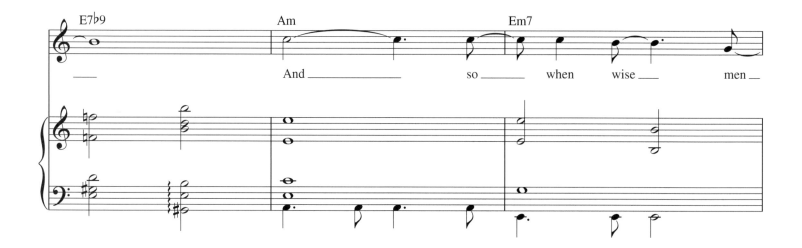

And so when wise men

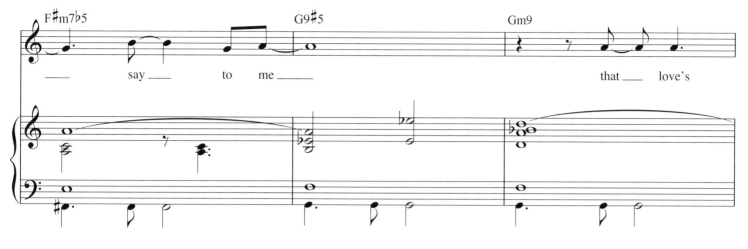

say ___ to me ___ that ___ love's

young dream nev - er ___ comes true, ___

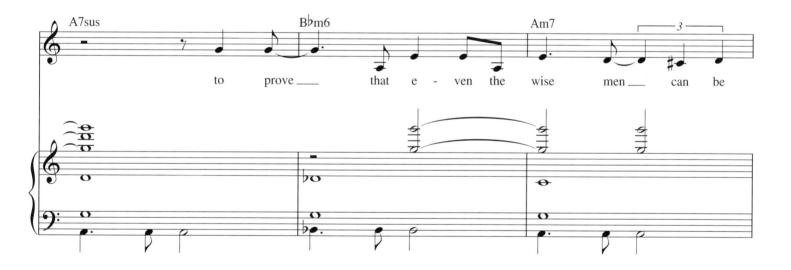

to prove ___ that e - ven the wise men ___ can be

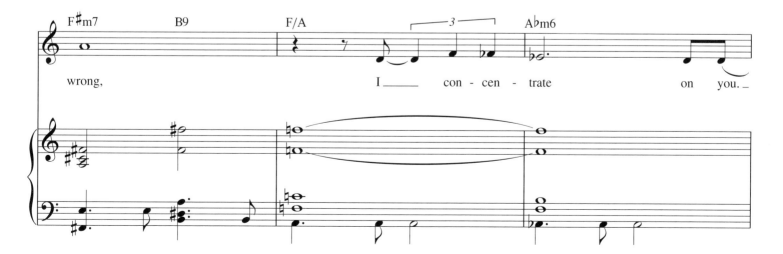

wrong, I ___ con - cen - trate on you. ___

98

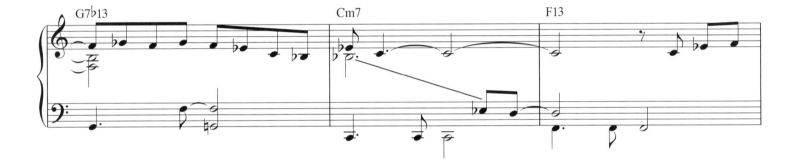

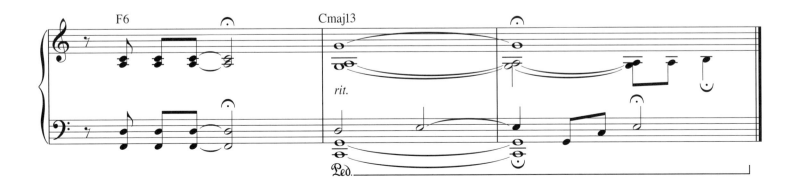

I HADN'T ANYONE TILL YOU

Words and Music by
RAY NOBLE

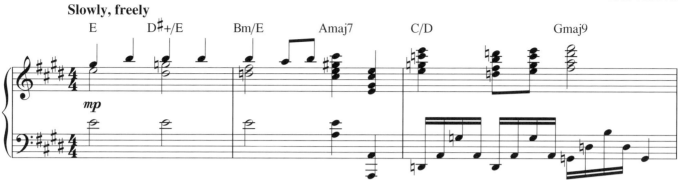

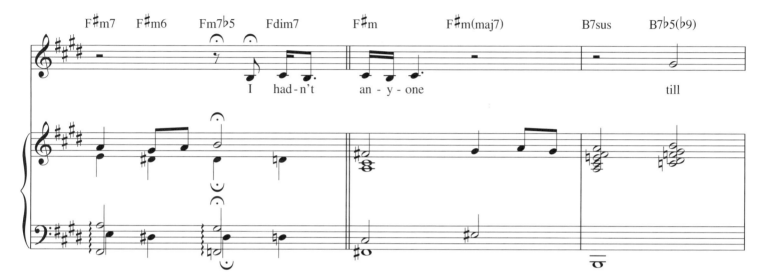

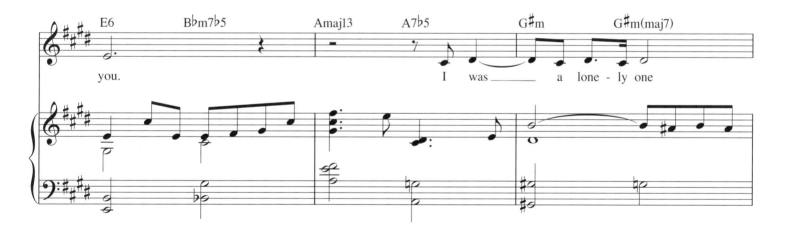

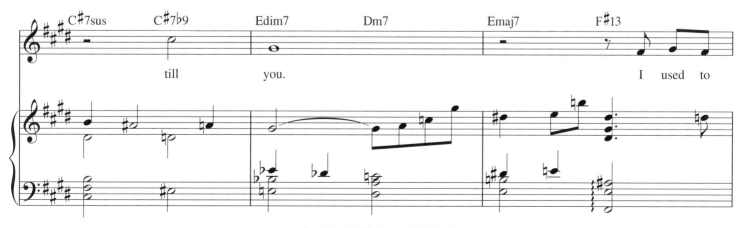

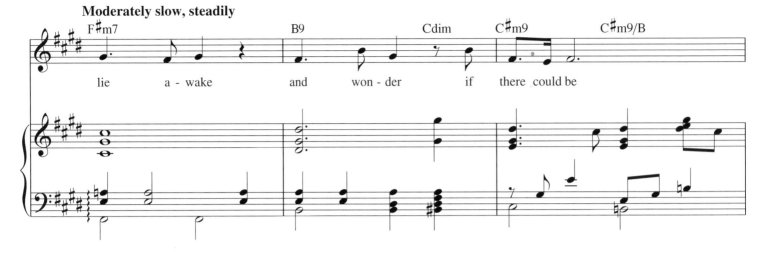

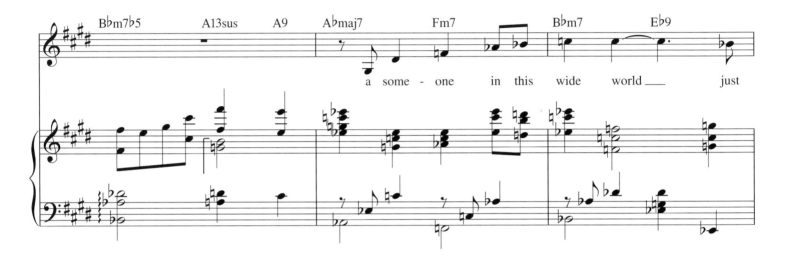

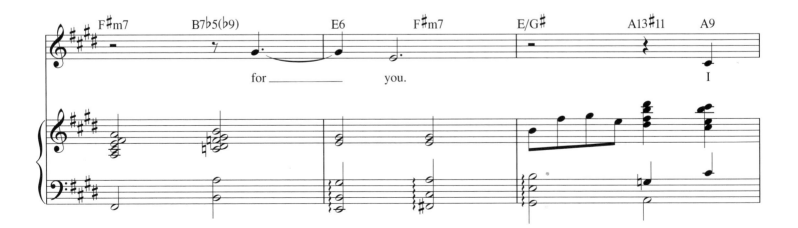

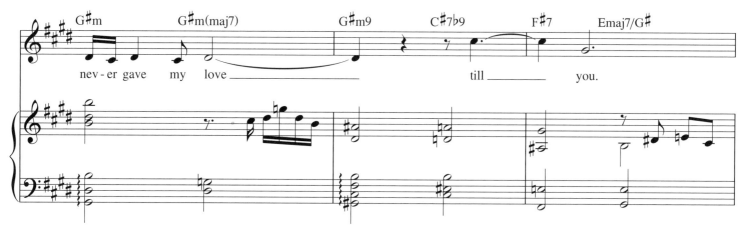

nev - er gave my love _____ till _____ you.

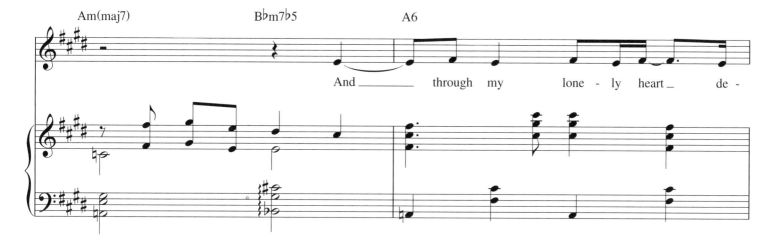

And _____ through my lone - ly heart ___ de -

mand - ing it, Cu - pid _____ took a hand _____

___ in it. I had - n't _____ an - y - one ___

102

till you.

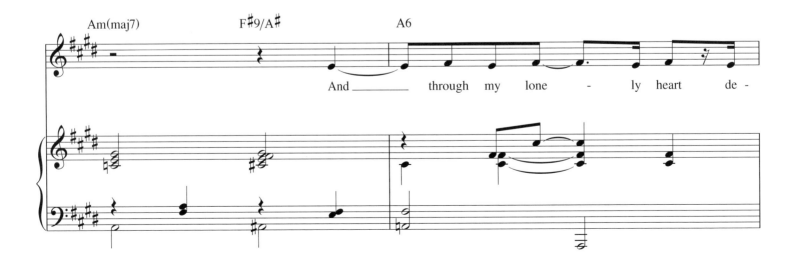

And _____ through my lone - ly heart de -

mand - ing it, Cu - pid took a hand in it. _____

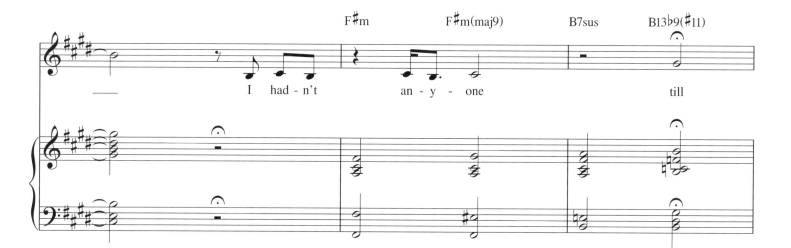

_____ I had - n't an - y - one till

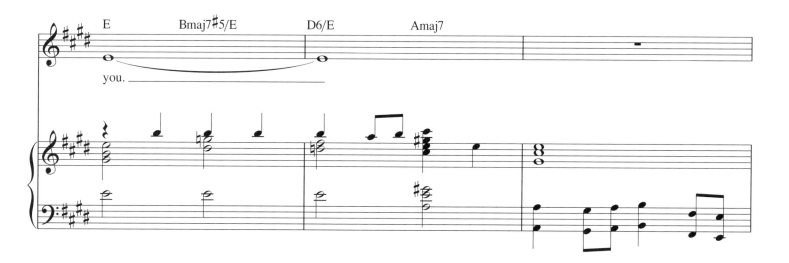

you. _____

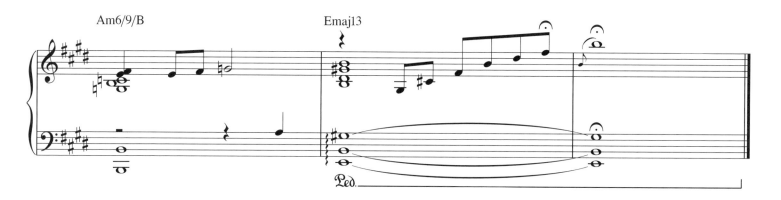

I COULD WRITE A BOOK

from PAL JOEY

Words by LORENZ HART
Music by RICHARD RODGERS

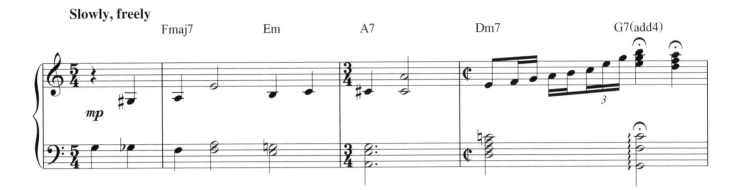

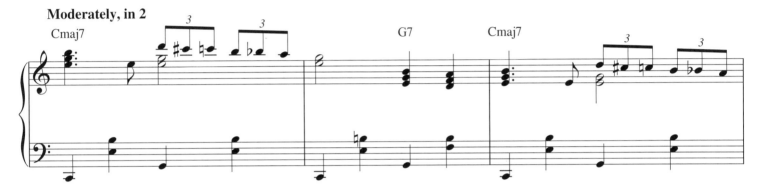

If they asked me, I could write a

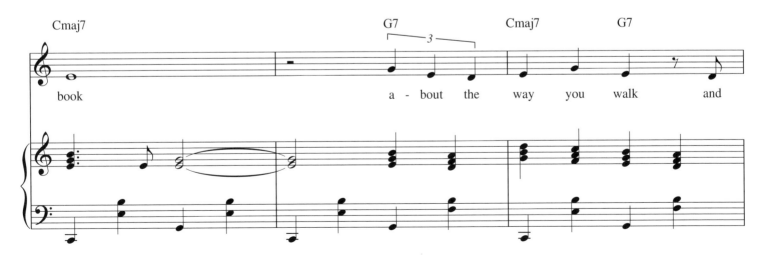

book a - bout the way you walk and

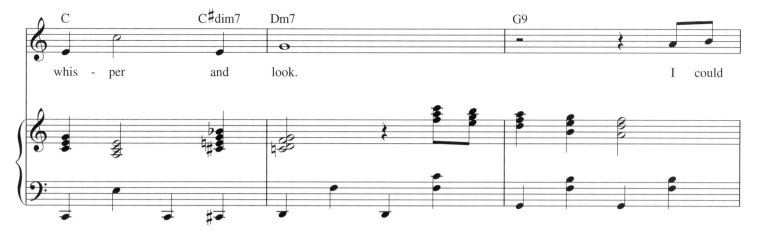

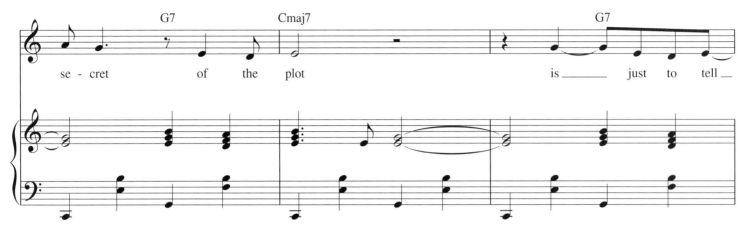

se - cret of the plot is _____ just to tell _____

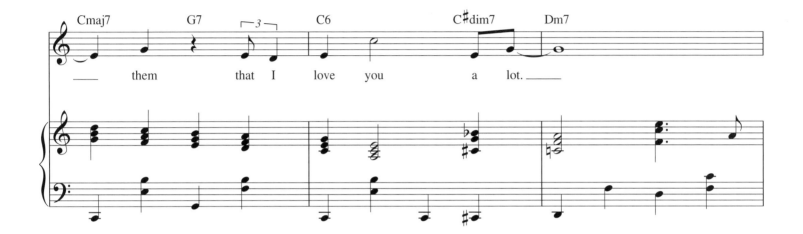

____ them that I love you a lot. _____

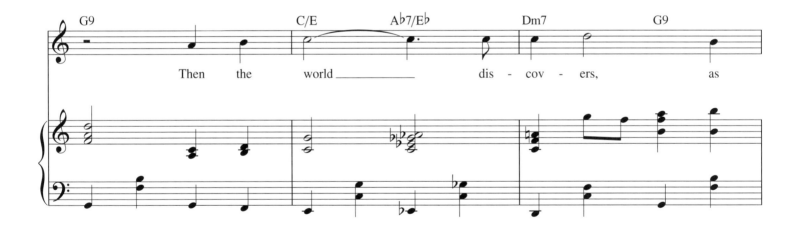

Then the world _____ dis - cov - ers, as

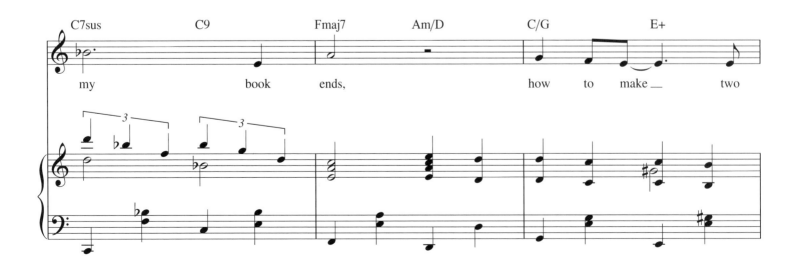

my book ends, how to make __ two

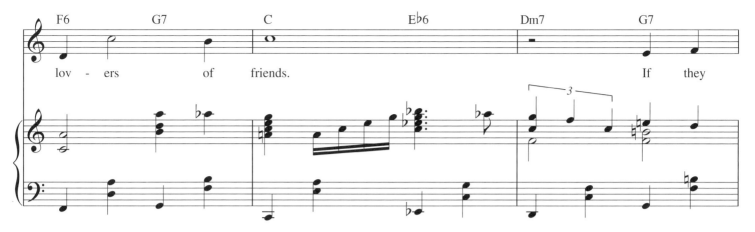

lov - ers   of   friends.   If   they

Swing $(\;\s♪\;\;=\;\;\overset{3}{\sqcap}\;)$

asked   me, _____   I   could   write   a   book ___

a - bout   the   way ___   you   walk ___   and   whis - per   and   look. _

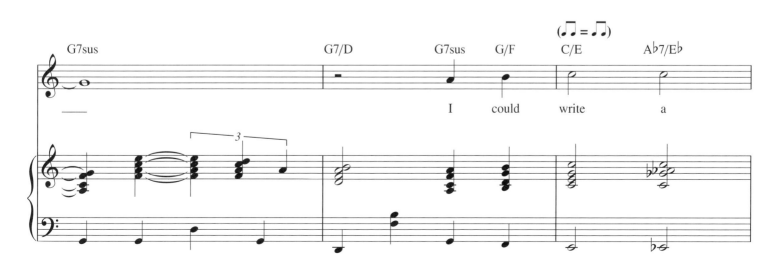

$(\;\sqcap\;=\;\sqcap\;)$

___   I   could   write   a

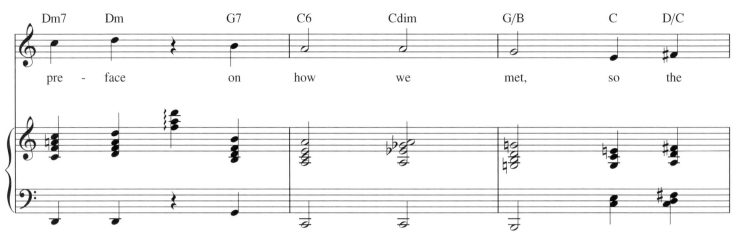

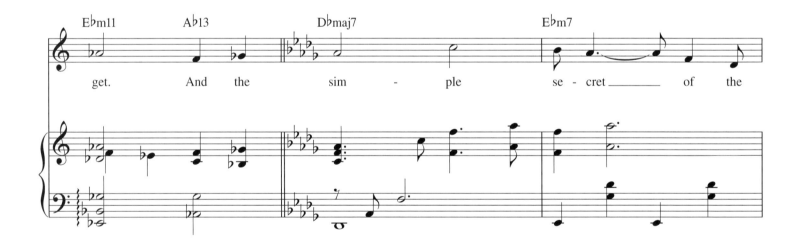

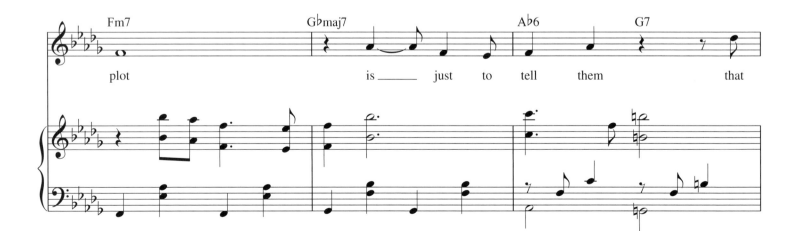

I ___ love ___ you a lot. ___ Then the

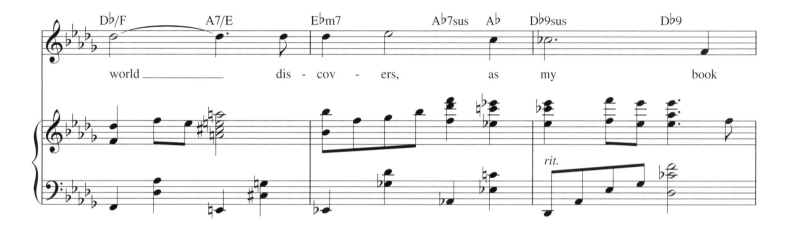

world ___ dis - cov - ers, as my book

Slowly, freely

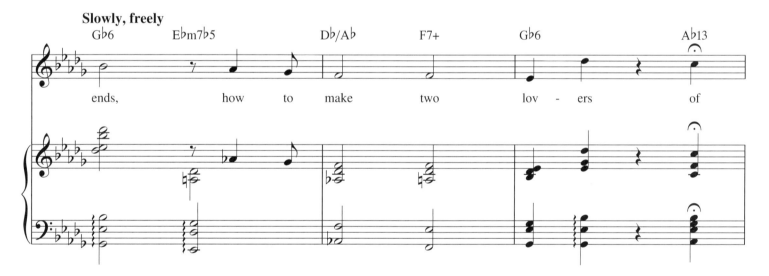

ends, how to make two lov - ers of

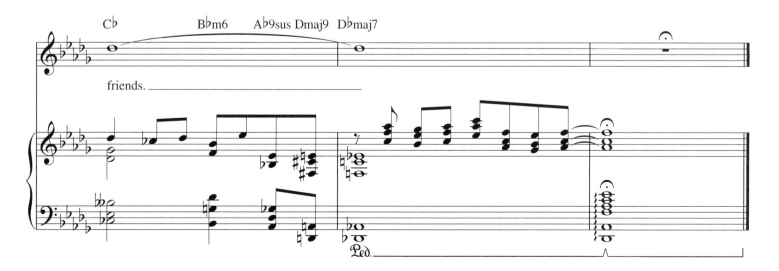

friends. ___

I LOVE PARIS

Words and Music by
COLE PORTER

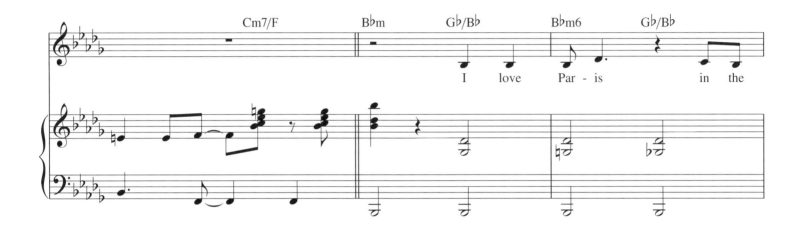

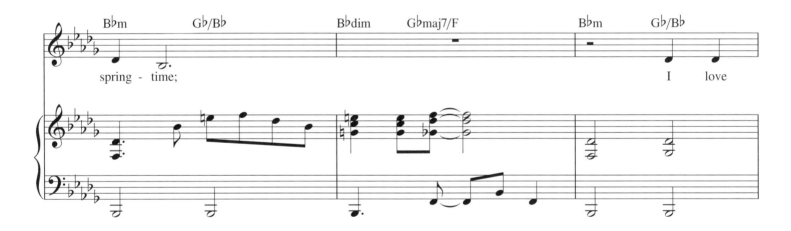

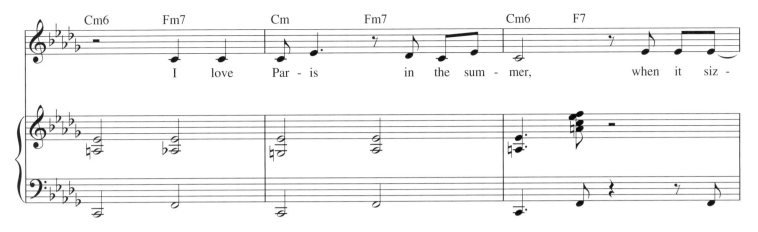

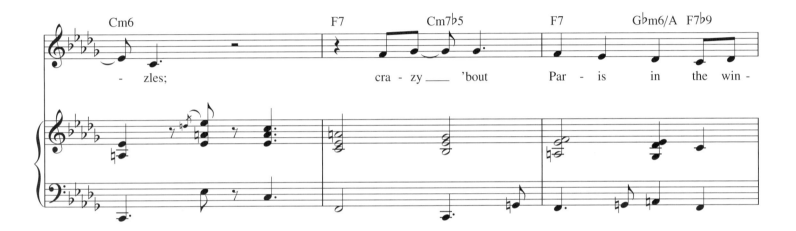

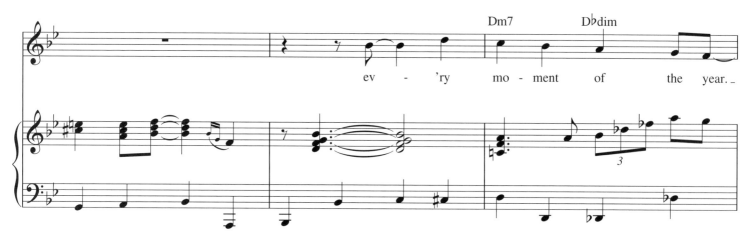

ev - 'ry mo - ment of the year.

I ___ love

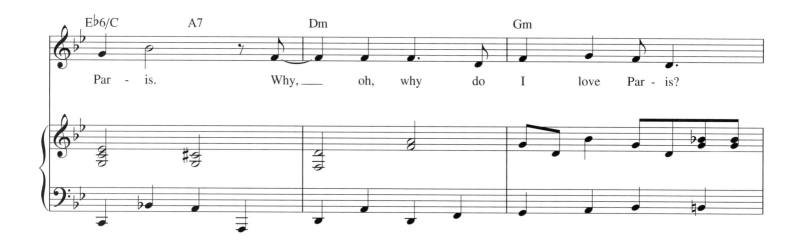

Par - is. Why, ___ oh, why do I love Par - is?

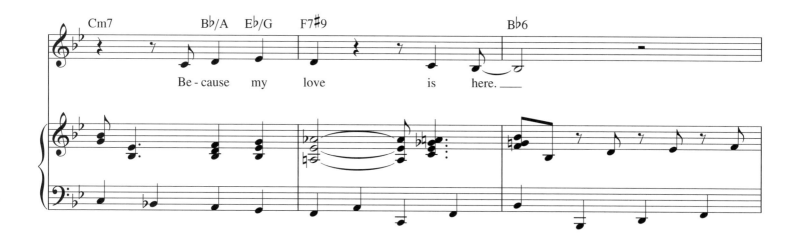

Be - cause my love is here. ___

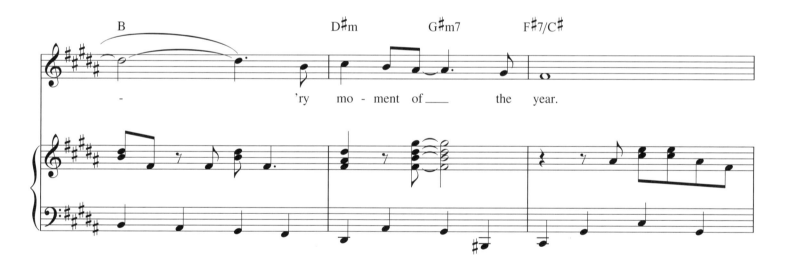

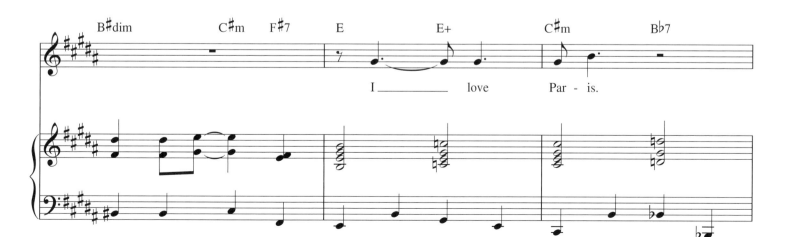

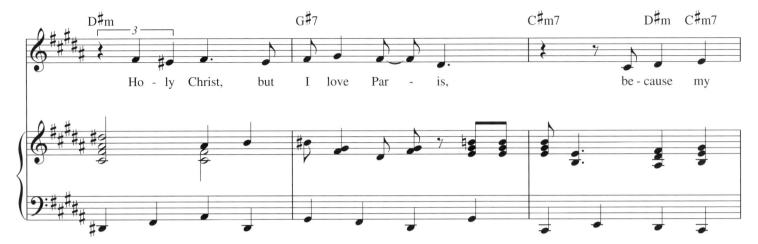

Ho - ly Christ, but I love Par - is, be - cause my

love is here. She's

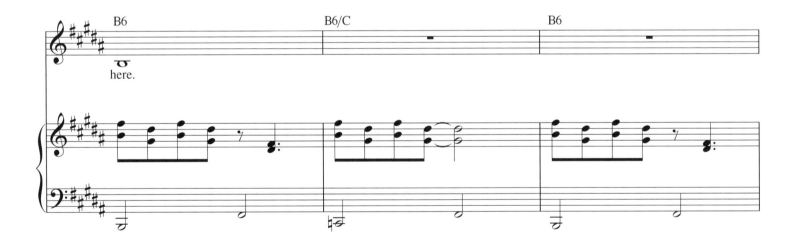

here.

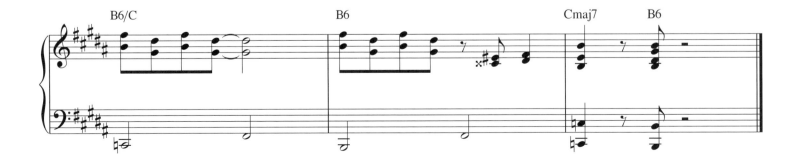

ISLE OF CAPRI

Words and Music by JAMES KENNEDY
and WILHELM GROSZ

Moderate Swing

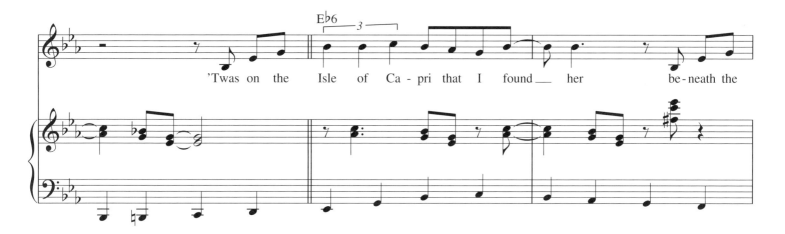

'Twas on the Isle of Ca-pri that I found ___ her be-neath the

shade of an old ___ wal-nut tree. Oh, I can

still see the flow'rs ___ bloom-ing 'round ___ her where we met,

on the Isle ___ of Ca - pri. ___

Cha Cha (♩♩ = ♩♩)

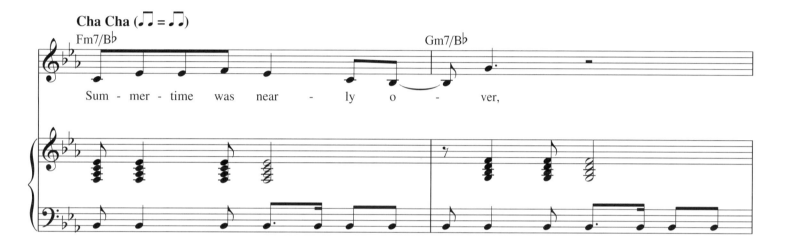

Sum - mer - time was near - ly o - ver,

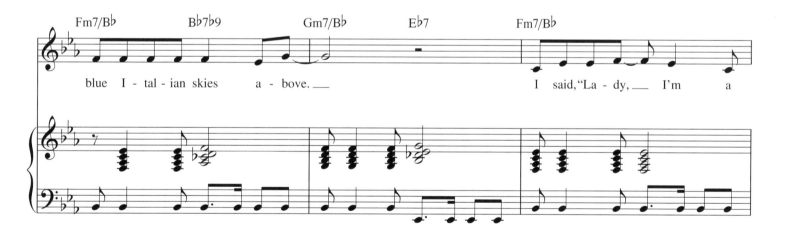

blue I - tal - ian skies a - bove. ___ I said, "La - dy, ___ I'm a

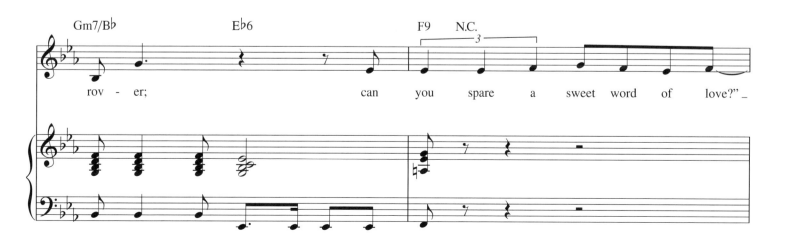

rov - er; can you spare a sweet word of love?" _

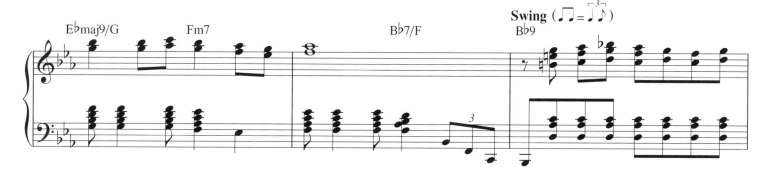

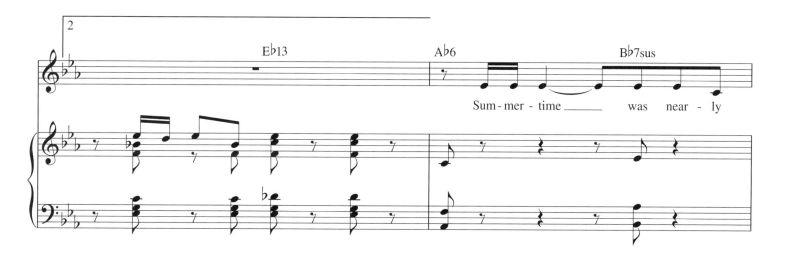

Sum - mer - time _____ was near - ly

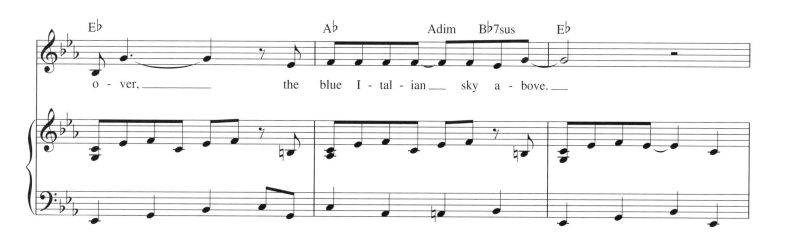

o - ver, _____ the blue I - tal - ian ___ sky a - bove. __

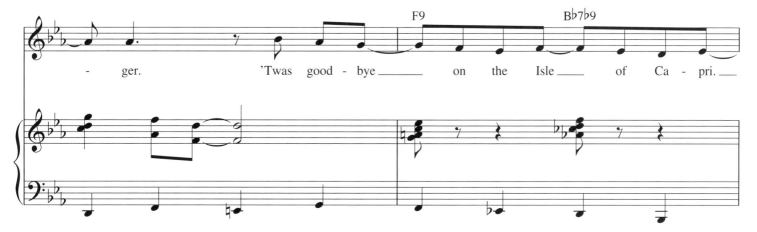

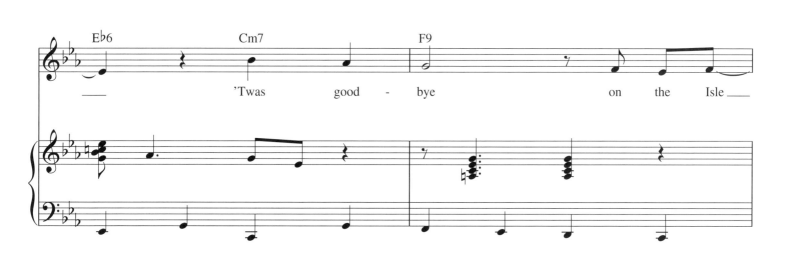

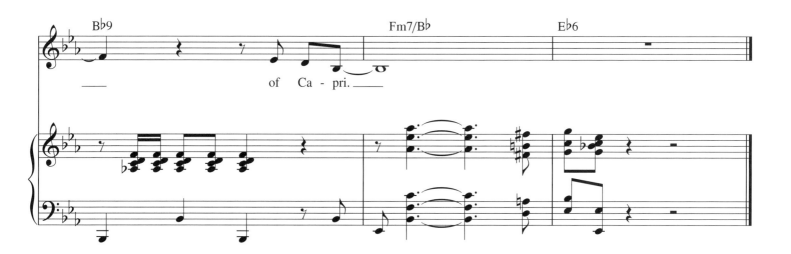

I'M GLAD THERE IS YOU
(In This World of Ordinary People)

Words and Music by PAUL MADEIRA
and JIMMY DORSEY

Moderate Ballad

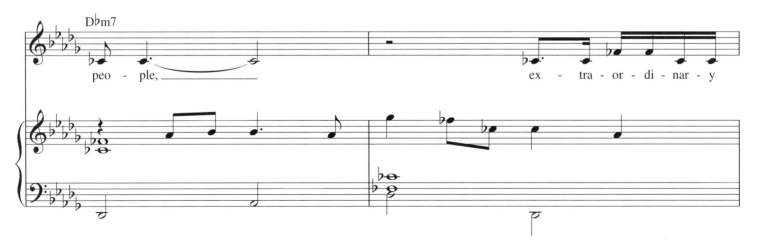

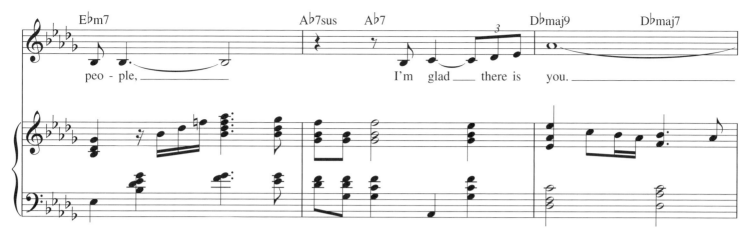

peo - ple, _____ I'm glad ___ there is you. _____

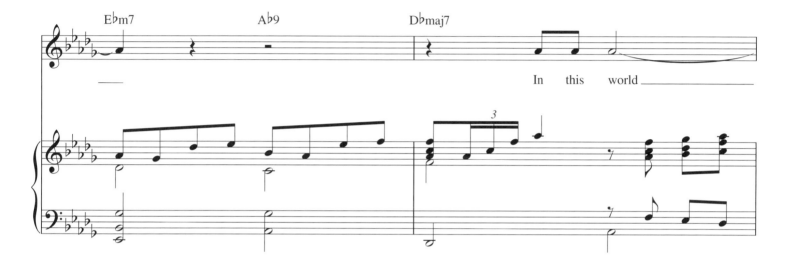

_____ In this world _____

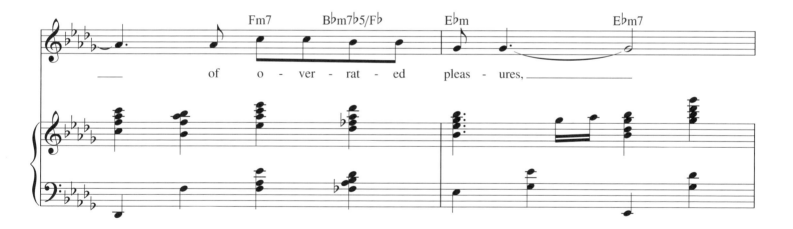

_____ of o - ver - rat - ed pleas - ures, _____

of _____ un - der - rat - ed treas - ures, _____

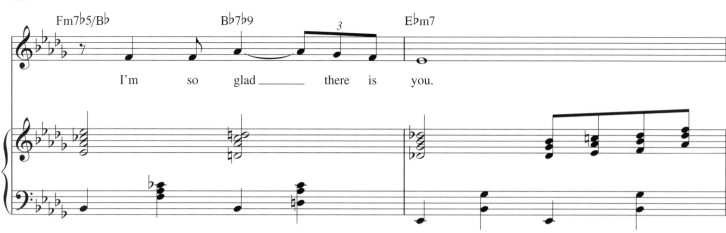

I'm so glad _____ there is you.

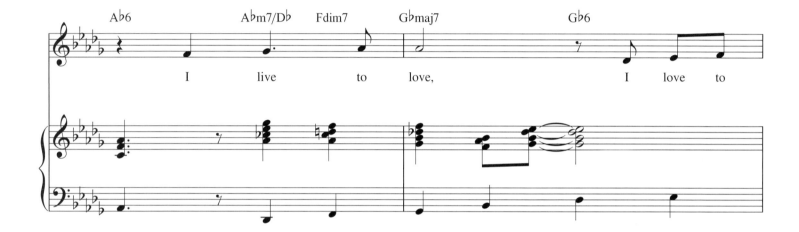

I live to love, I love to

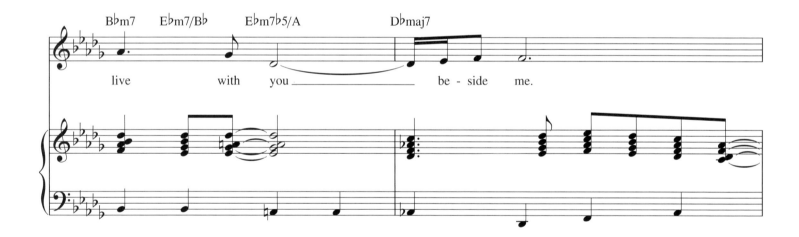

live with you _____ be - side me.

This role's so new; I'll _____ mud - dle

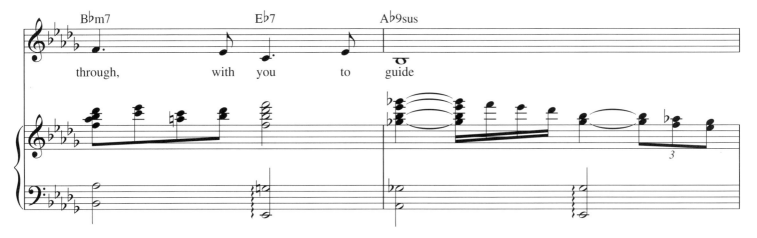

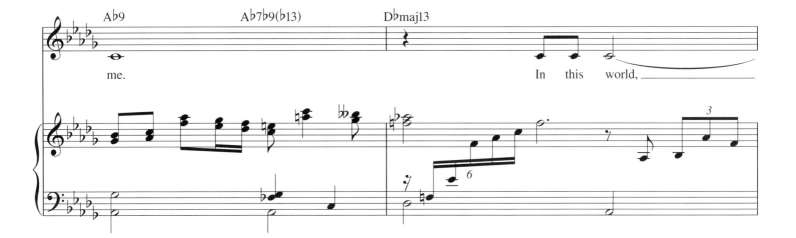

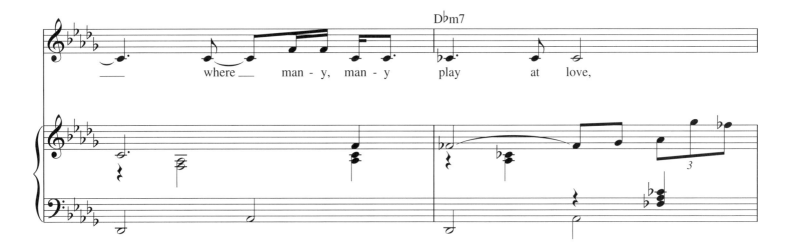

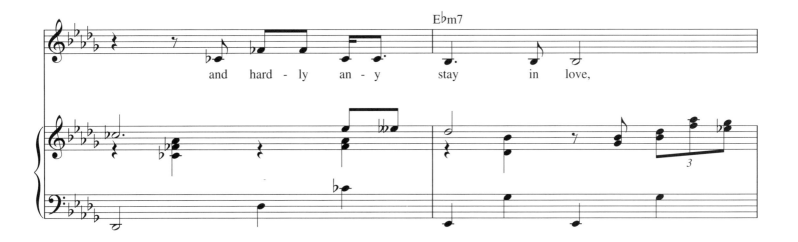

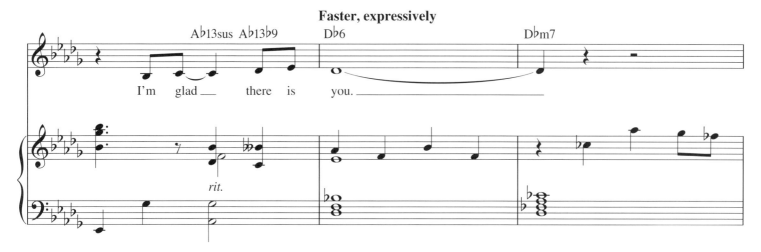

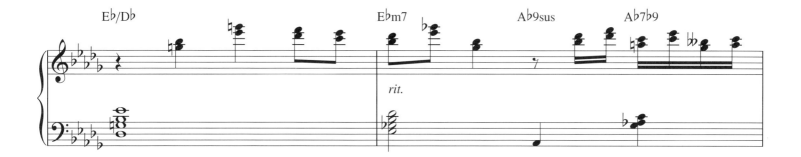

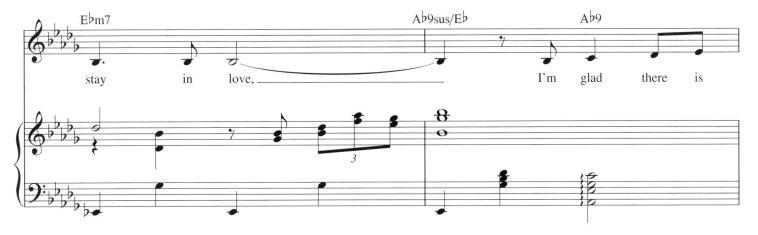

stay in love, _____ I'm glad there is

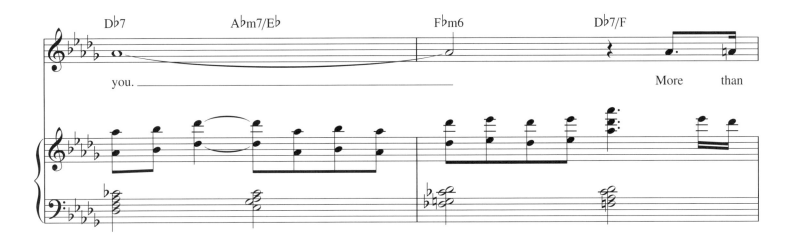

you. _____ More than

Freely, expressively

ev - er, _____ I'm glad there is you. _____

IN THE WEE SMALL HOURS OF THE MORNING

Words by BOB HILLIARD
Music by DAVID MANN

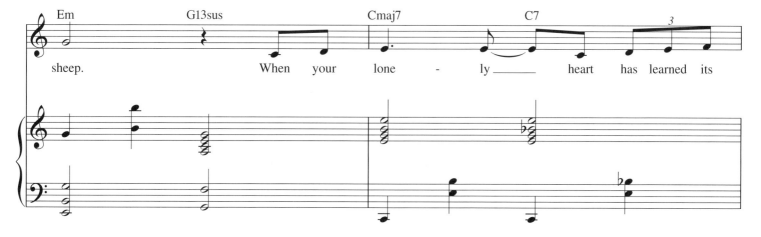

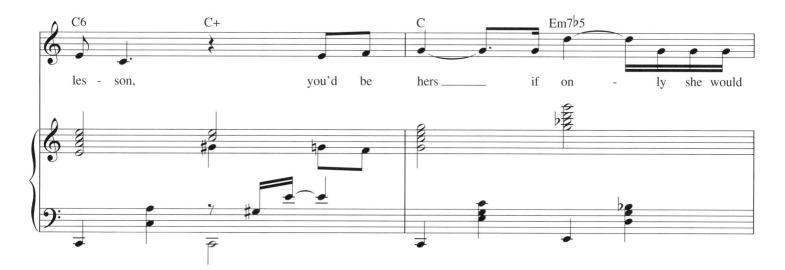

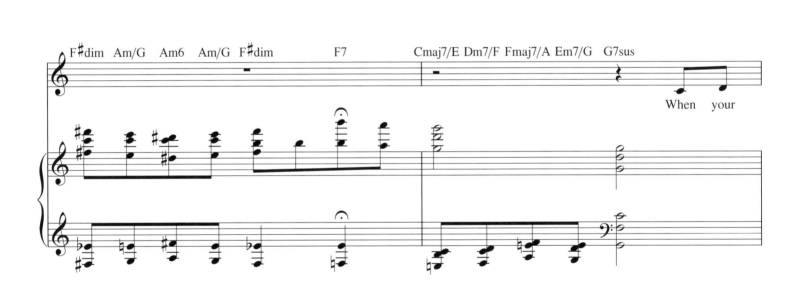

When your

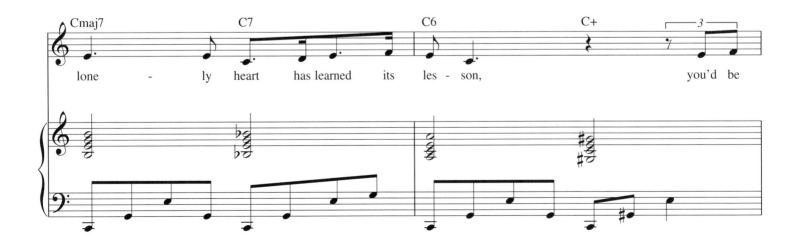

lone - ly heart has learned its les - son, you'd be

hers _____ if on - ly she would call. In the

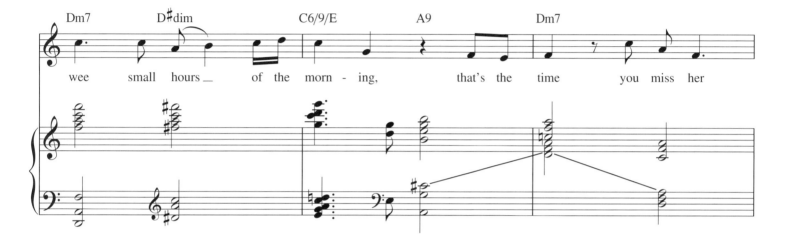

wee small hours __ of the morn - ing, that's the time you miss her

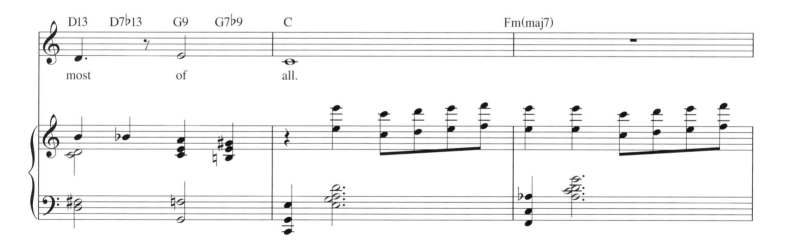

most of all.

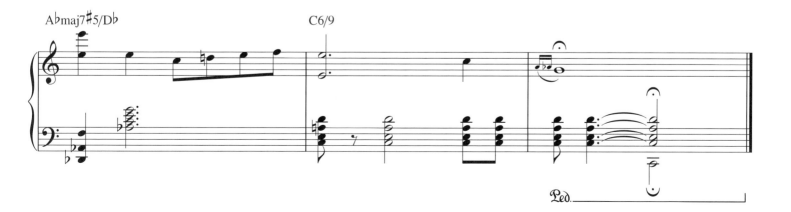

IT HAPPENED IN MONTEREY

Words by BILLY ROSE
Music by MABEL WAYNE

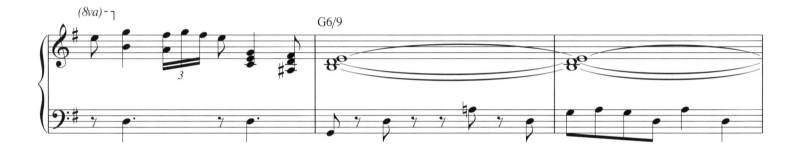

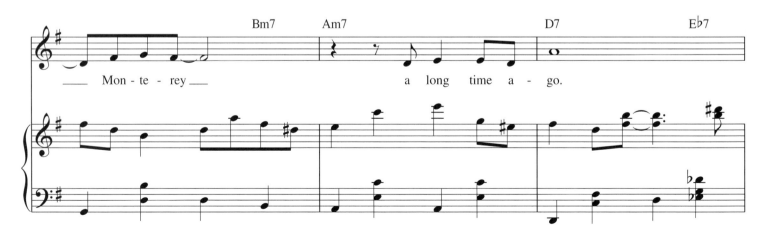

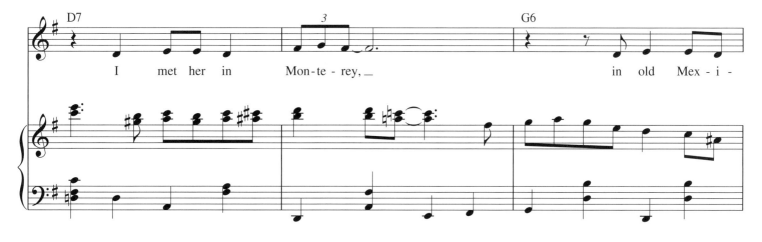

I met her in Mon-te-rey, __ in old Mex-i-

co. Stars __ and steel __ gui-tars, __ and lus-cious

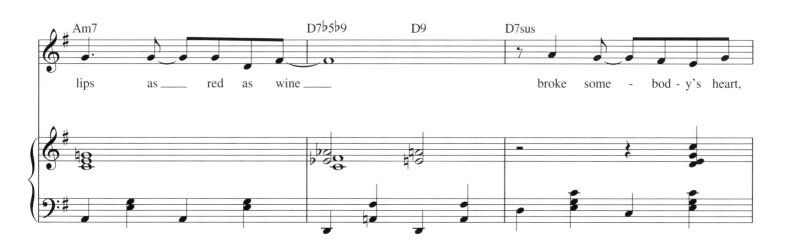

lips as __ red as wine __ broke some-bod-y's heart,

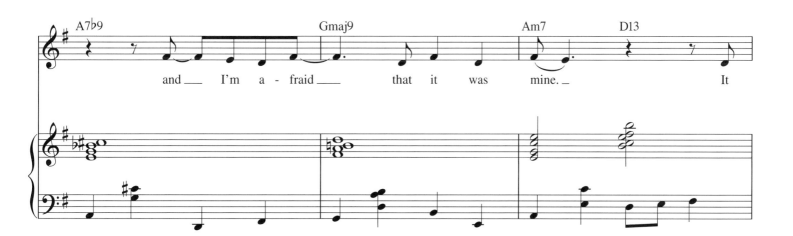

and __ I'm a-fraid __ that it was mine. __ It

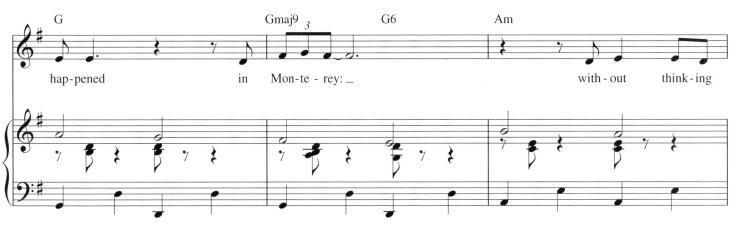

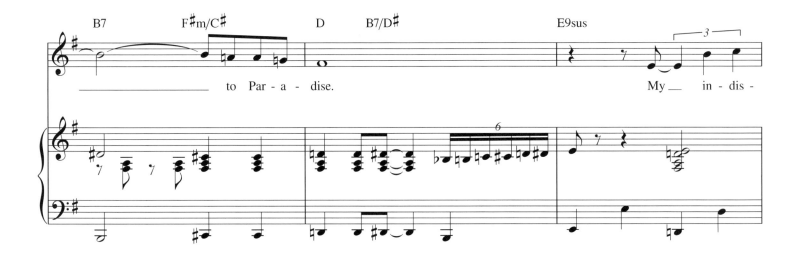

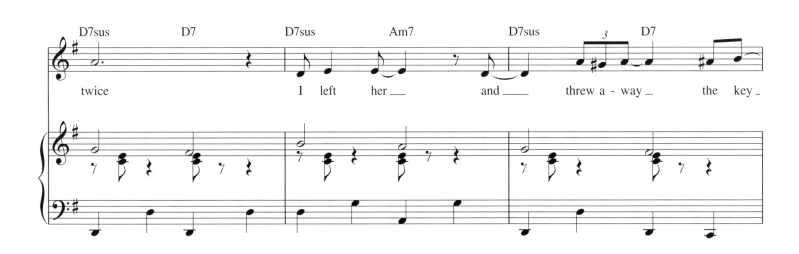

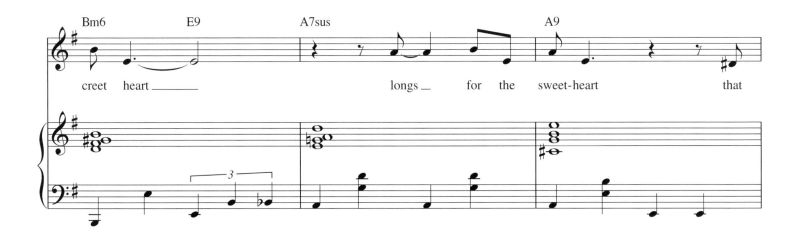

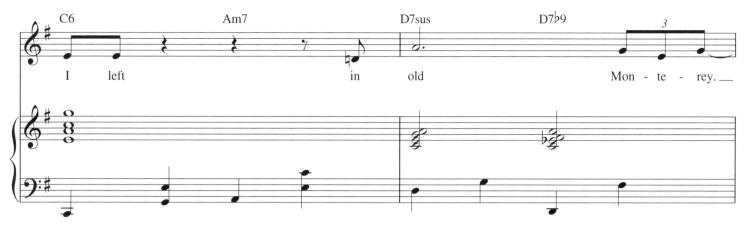

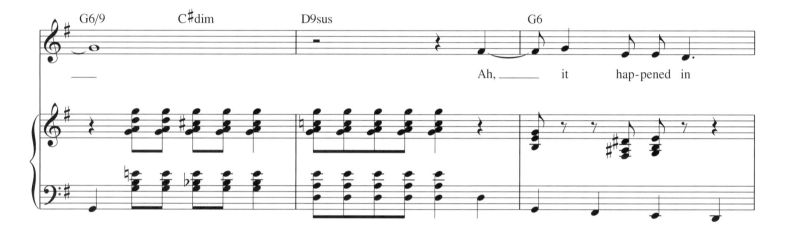

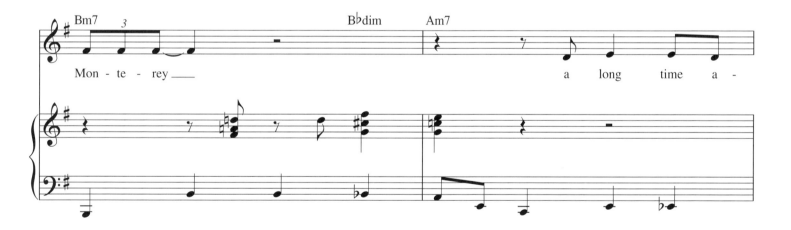

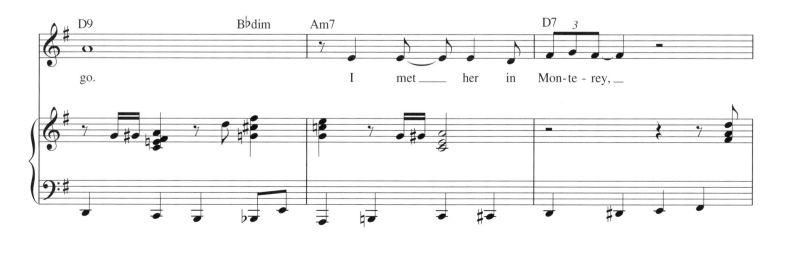

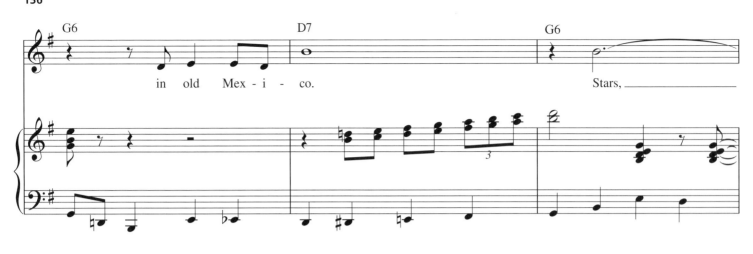

in old Mex - i - co.   Stars, _____

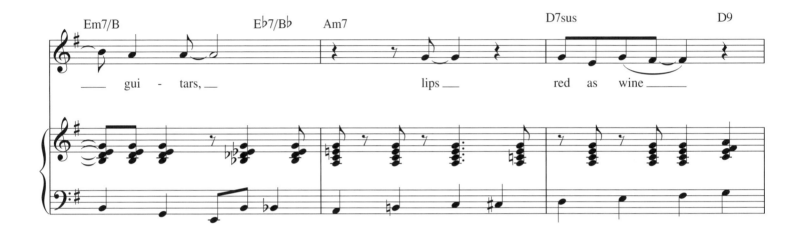

____ gui - tars, ____   lips ____   red as wine _____

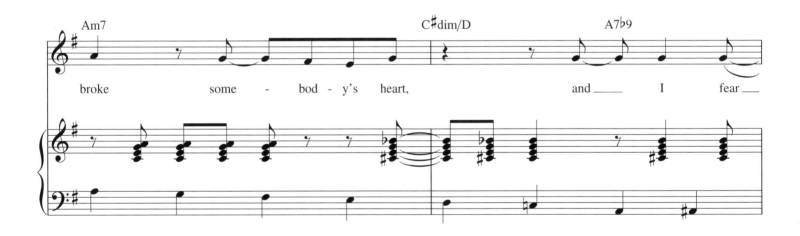

broke   some - bod - y's heart,   and ____ I   fear ____

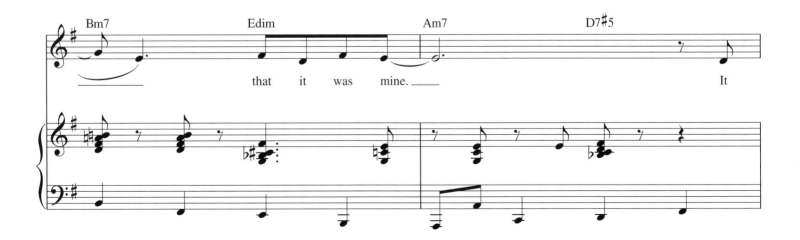

_____   that it was mine. ____   It

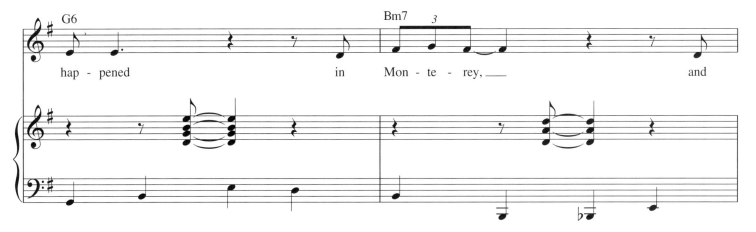

hap - pened   in   Mon - te - rey, ___   and

with - out   think - ing   twice, ___   I

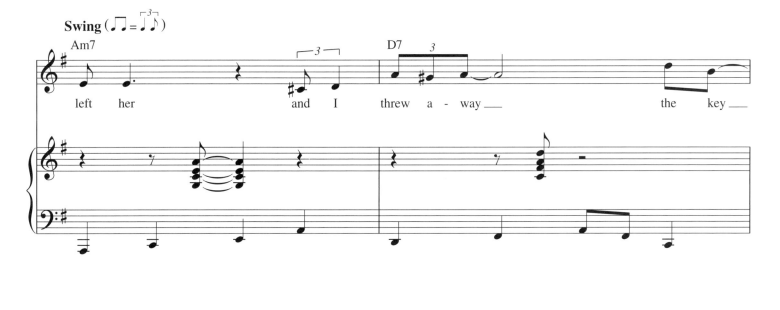

left her   and I   threw a - way ___   the key ___

___   to Par - a - dise.   My ___   in - dis -

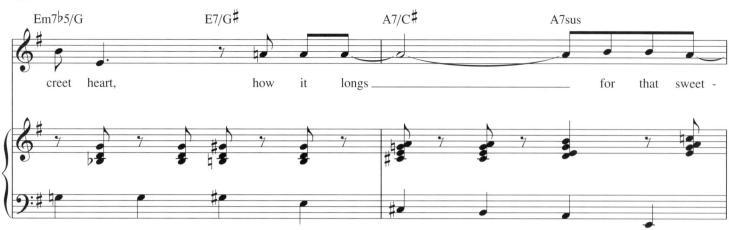

creet heart, how it longs _____ for that sweet -

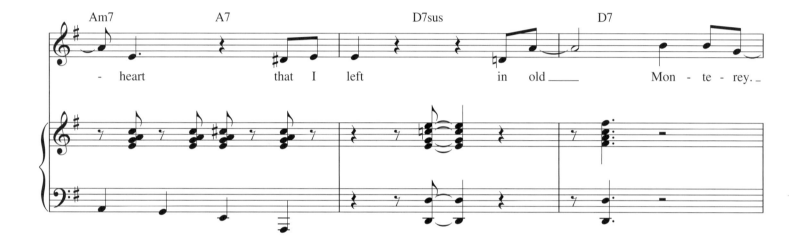

- heart that I left in old ____ Mon - te - rey. __

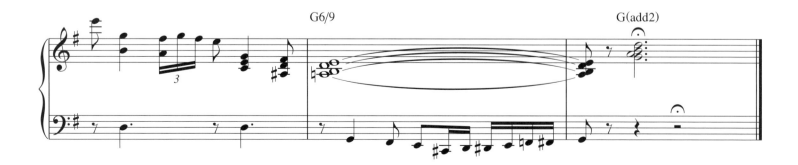

LEAN BABY

Lyric by ROY ALFRED
Music by BILLY MAY

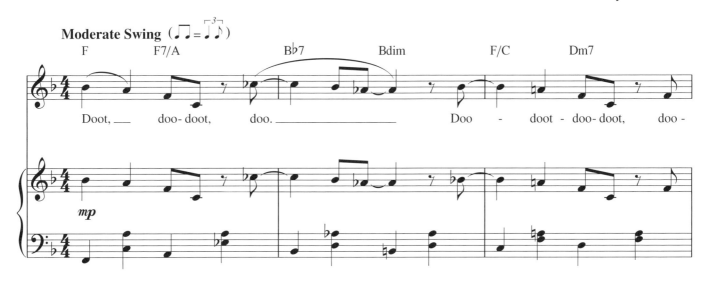

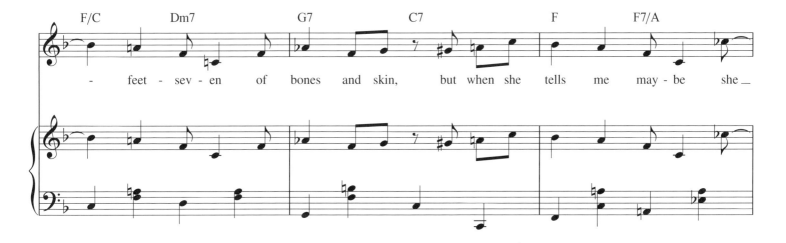

___ loves me, I feel as mel - low as a fel - low can be. ___

She's so skin - ny, she's ___ so drawn, when she stands side - ways you

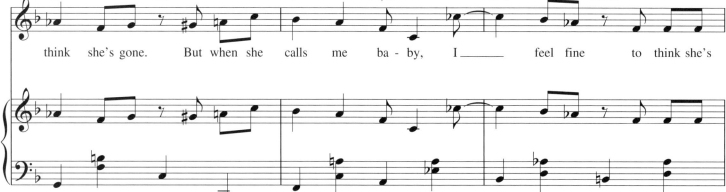

think she's gone. But when she calls me ba - by, I ___ feel fine to think she's

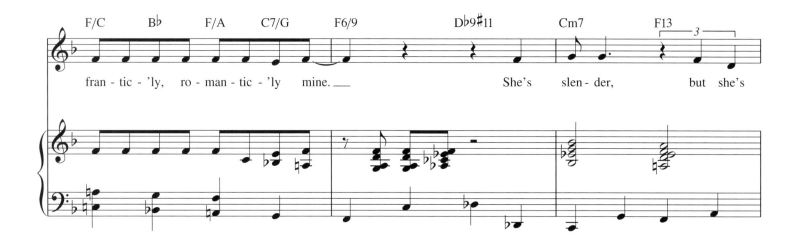

fran - tic - 'ly, ro - man - tic - 'ly mine. ___ She's slen - der, but she's

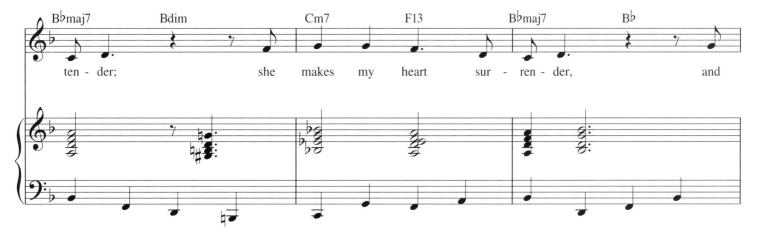

ten - der; she makes my heart sur - ren - der, and

ev - 'ry night, _ when I hold her tight, the feel - in' is nice: my arms can

go a - round _ twice. My lean ba - by, she's ___ so slim. A

broom - stick's wid - er, but not as trim, and when she starts to kiss ___ me, then ___

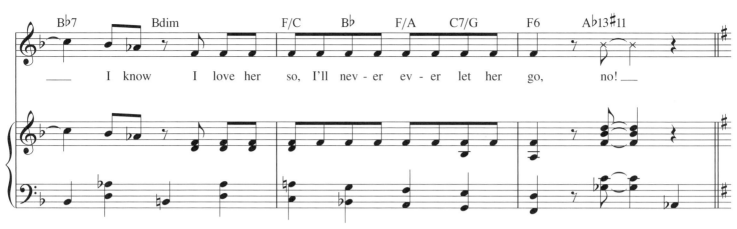

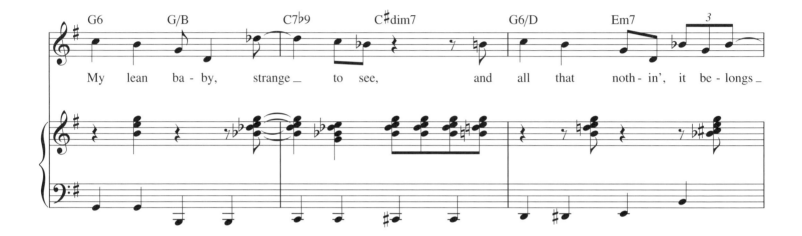

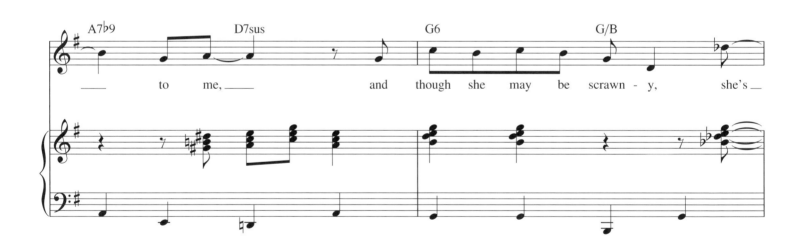

And ___ she's so skin-ny, she's ___ so drawn, when

she stands side - ways ___ you would think that she's gone. ___ But

when she calls me, ___ ba - by, I ___ feel fine ___ to think she's fran - tic - 'ly, ro - man - tic - 'ly mine. ___

I ___ chased her ___ and I caught her, then a

so, I'll nev-er ev-er let her go. My lean ba-by, tall __

__ and thin, doo-doot-doo-doot, doo-doo-doo-doo. Doo-doo-doo-

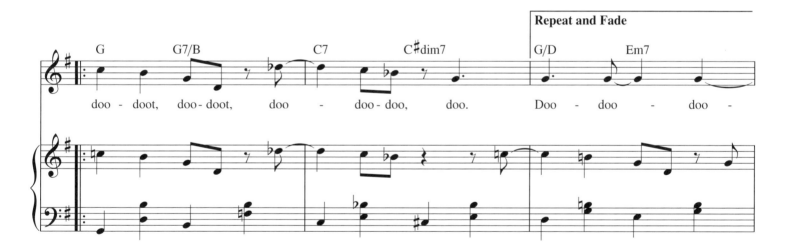

Repeat and Fade

doo-doot, doo-doot, doo - doo-doo, doo. Doo-doo-doo-

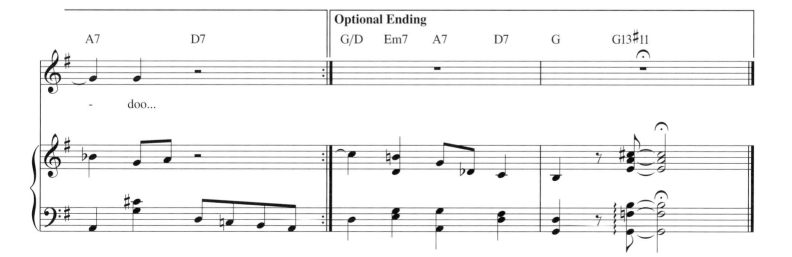

Optional Ending

- doo...

IT MIGHT AS WELL BE SPRING
from STATE FAIR

Lyrics by OSCAR HAMMERSTEIN II
Music by RICHARD RODGERS

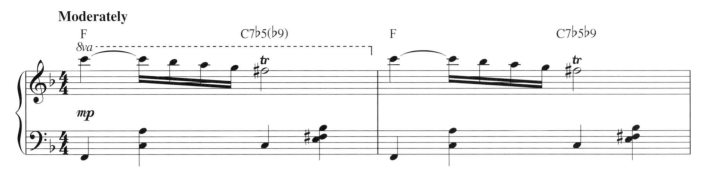

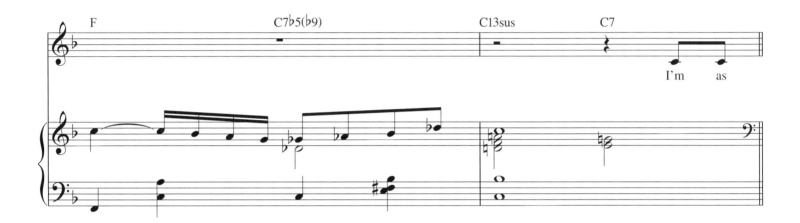

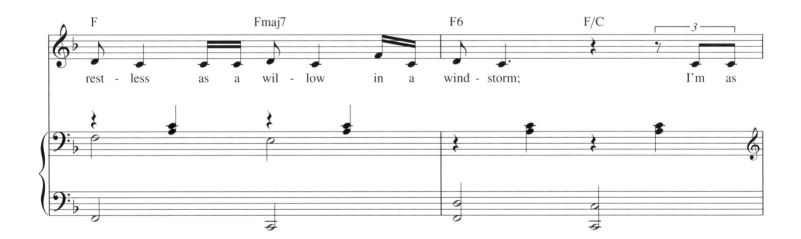

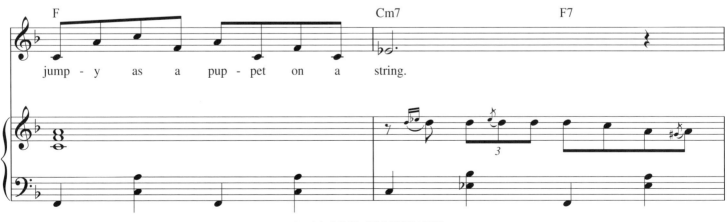

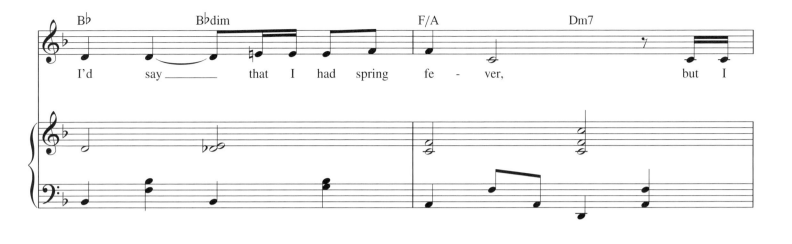

I'd say _____ that I had spring fe - ver, but I

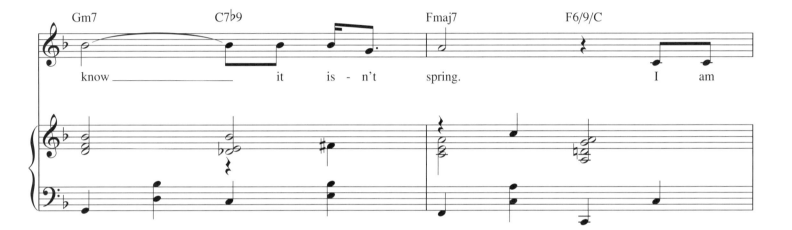

know _____ it is - n't spring. I am

star - ry - eyed, and vague - ly dis - con - tent - ed, like a

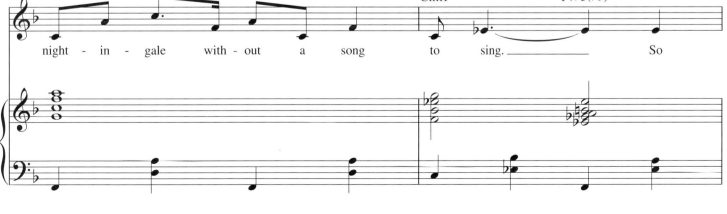

night - in - gale with - out a song to sing. _____ So

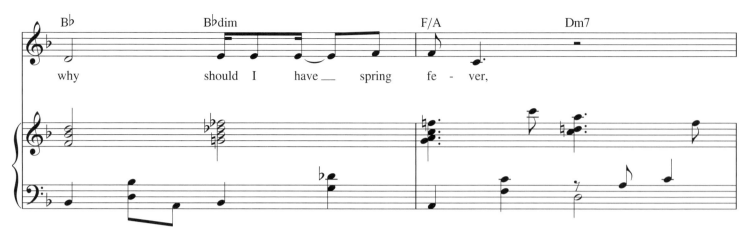

why should I have __ spring fe - ver,

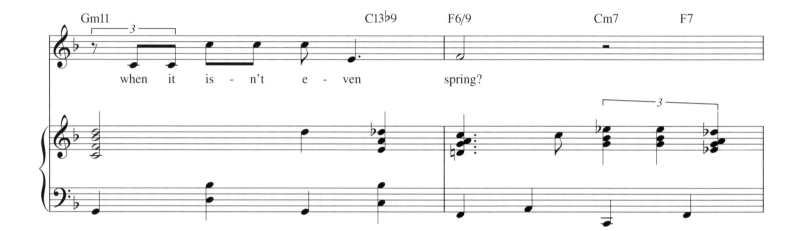

when it is - n't e - ven spring?

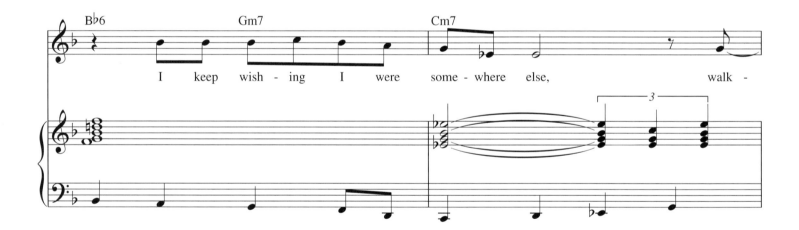

I keep wish - ing I were some - where else, walk -

- ing down a strange new street,

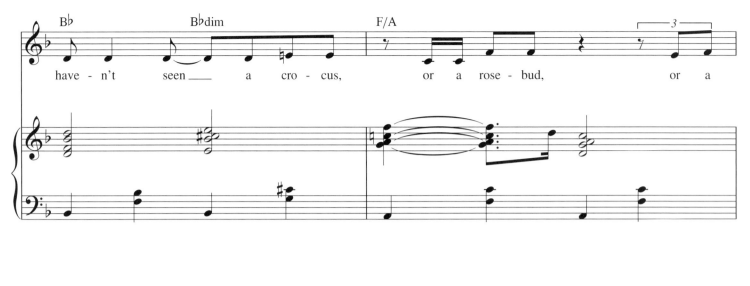

Bb   Bbdim   F/A

have - n't   seen _____ a   cro - cus,   or   a   rose - bud,   or   a

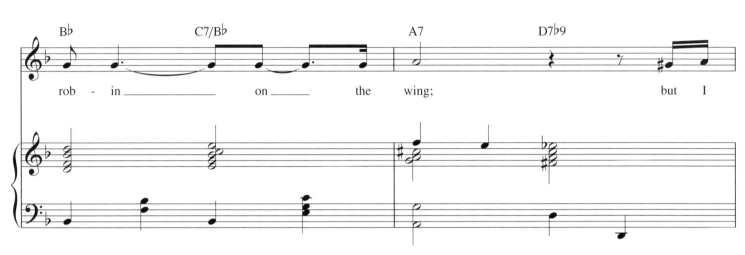

Bb   C7/Bb   A7   D7b9

rob - in _____ on _____ the   wing;   but   I

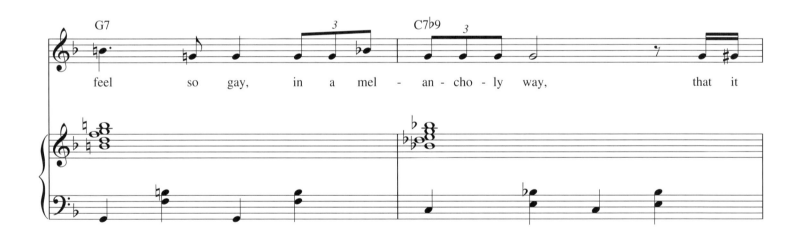

G7   C7b9

feel   so   gay,   in   a   mel - an - cho - ly   way,   that   it

F7   G7

might   as   well _____ be   spring.   It

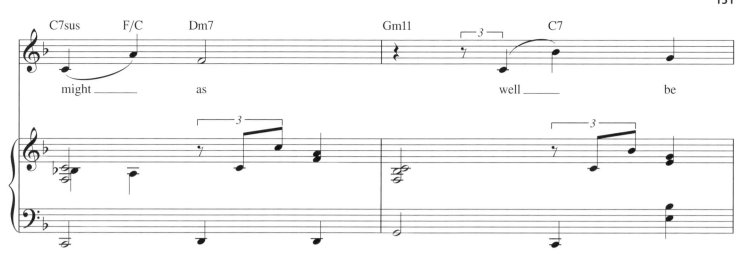

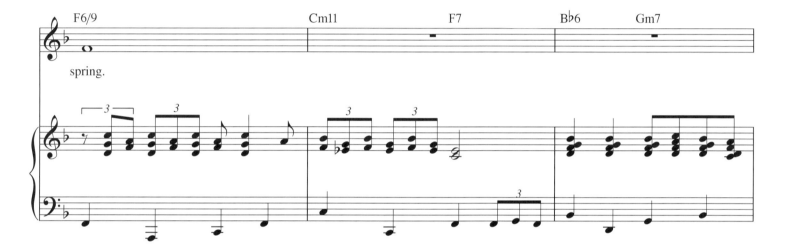

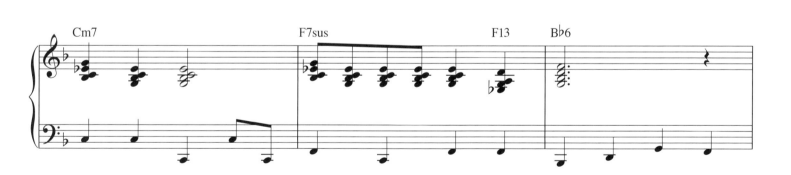

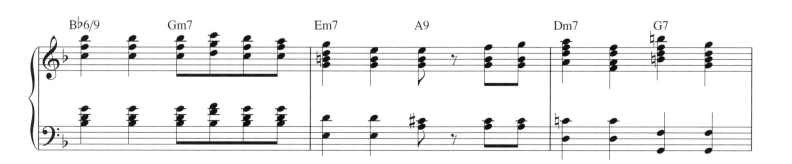

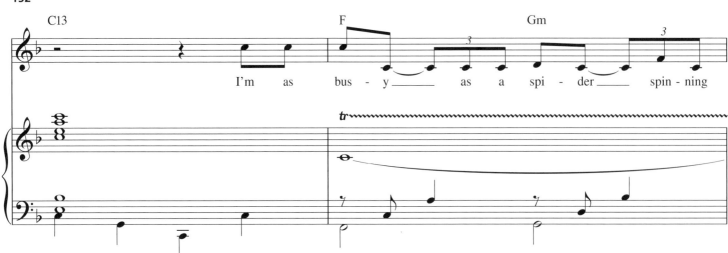

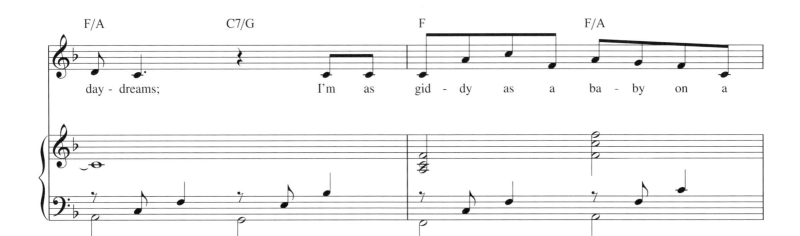

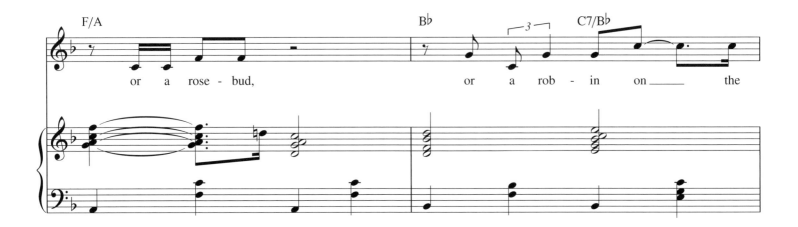

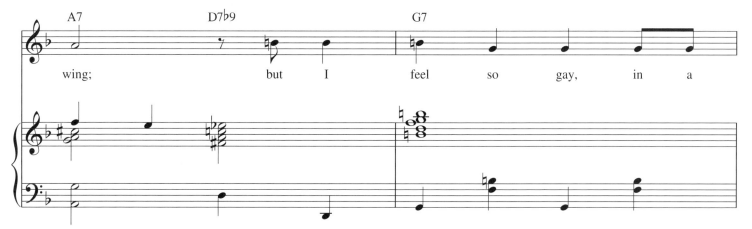

wing; but I feel so gay, in a

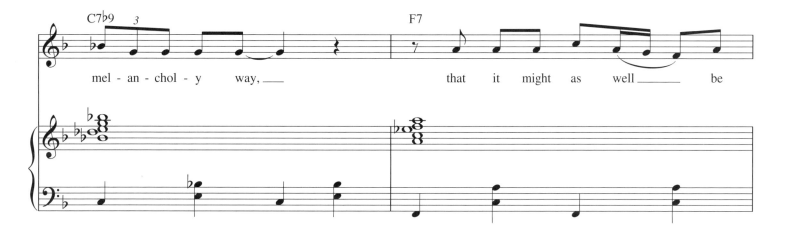

mel - an - chol - y way, ___ that it might as well ___ be

Slowly, freely

spring. It might ___ as well ___ be

spring. ___

LUCK BE A LADY
from GUYS AND DOLLS

By FRANK LOESSER

They call you "La - dy Luck," but

there is room for doubt. At times you'll have a

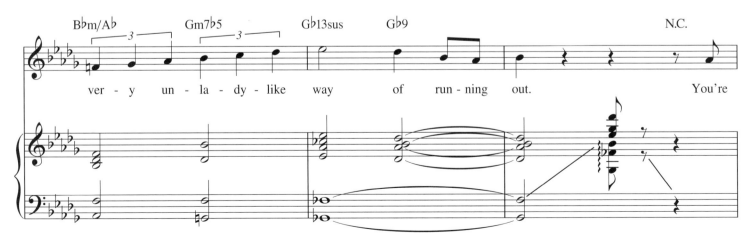

ver - y un - la - dy - like way of run - ning out. You're

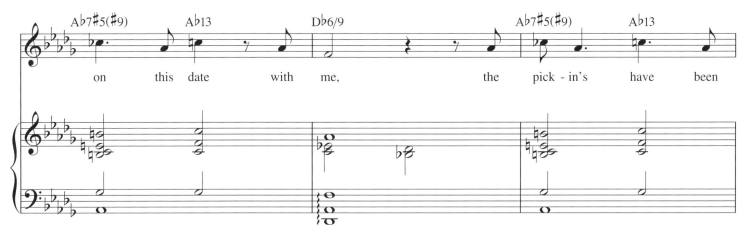

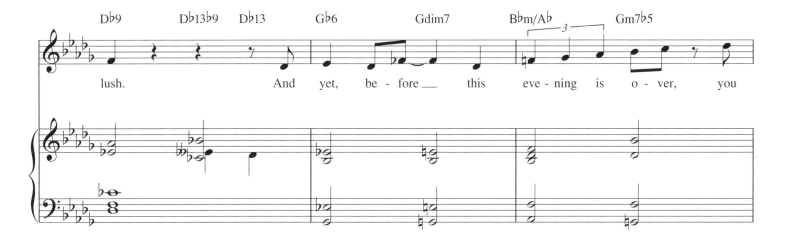

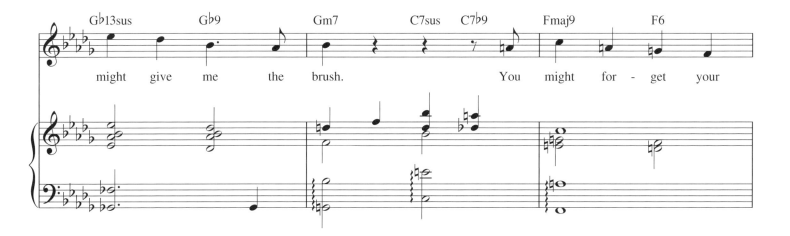

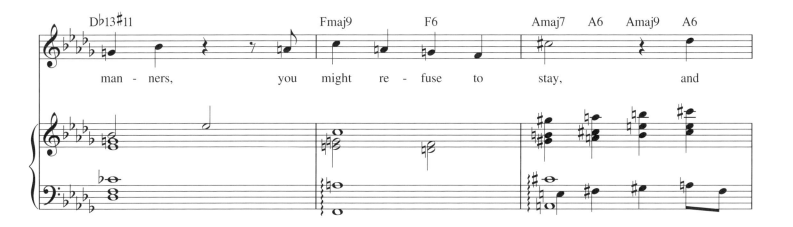

Moderately fast Swing

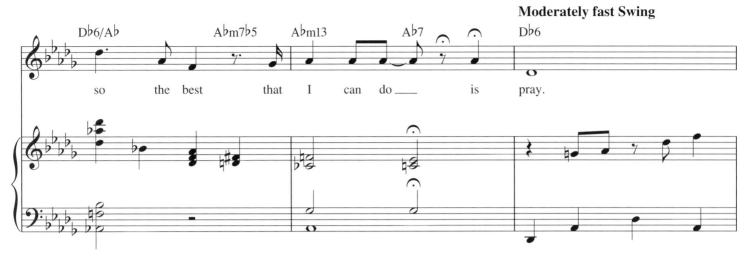

so the best that I can do _____ is pray.

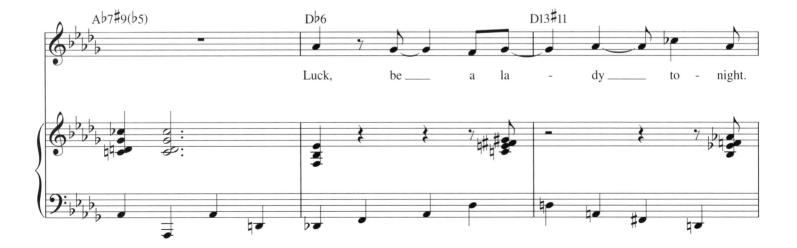

Luck, be _____ a la - dy _____ to - night.

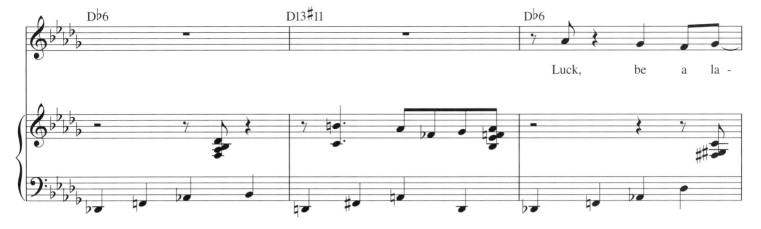

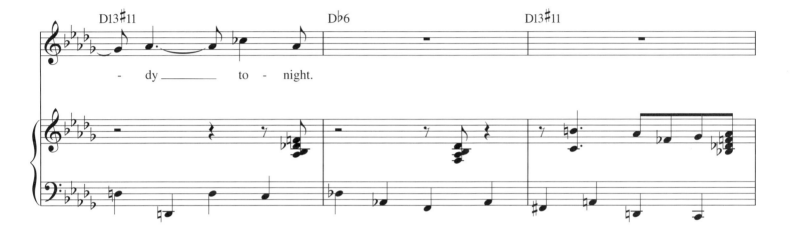

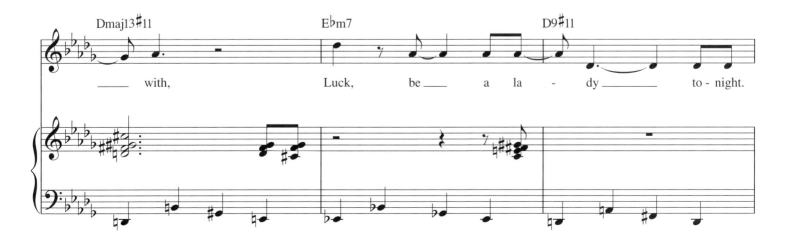

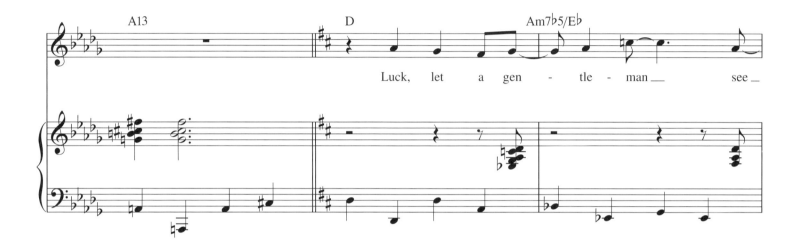

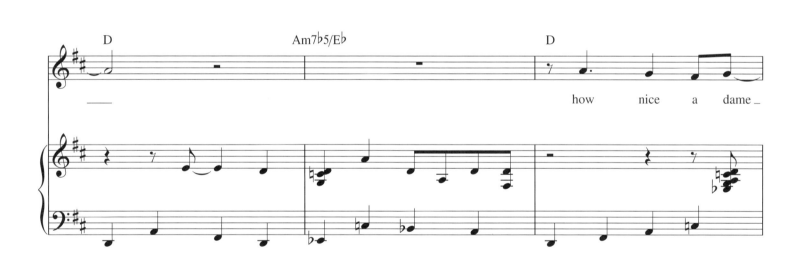

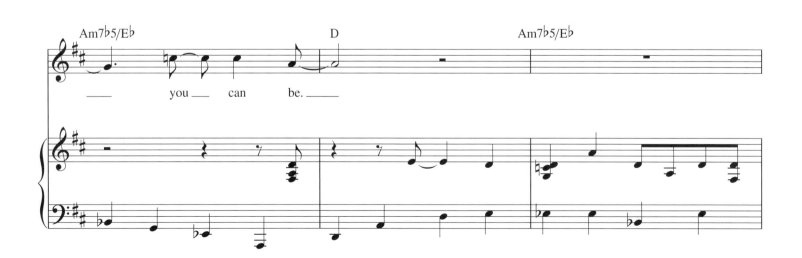

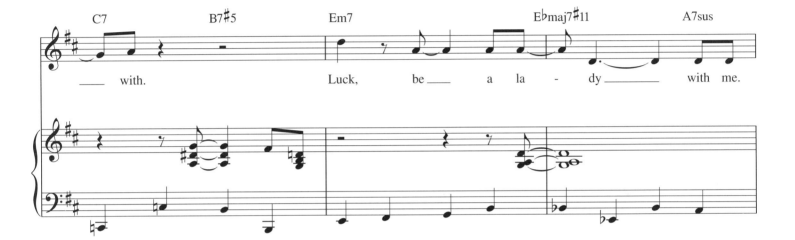

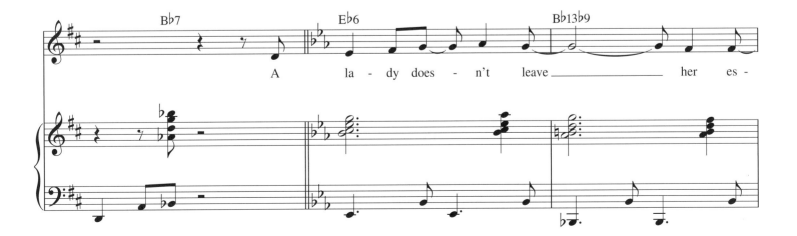

-cort. It is-n't fair; it is-n't nice.

A

la-dy does-n't wan-der all o-ver the room

and blow on some oth-er guy's dice.

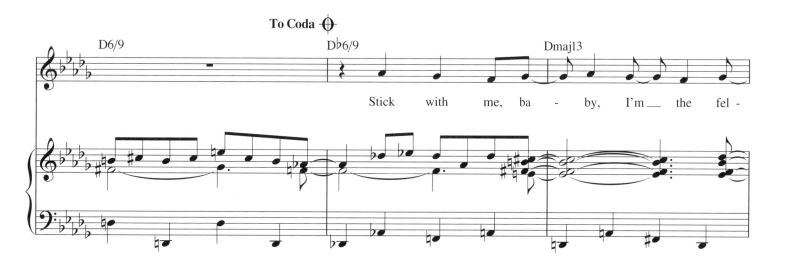

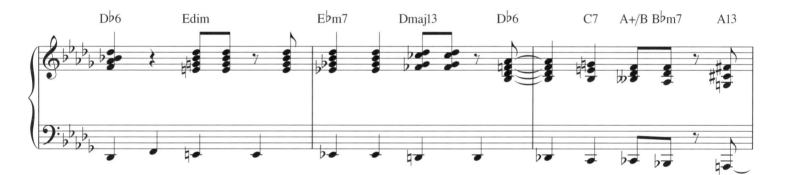

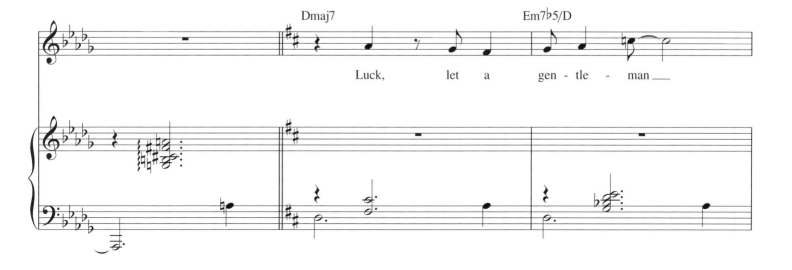

Luck, let a gen - tle - man ___

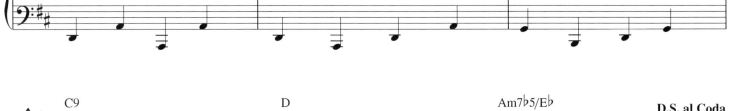

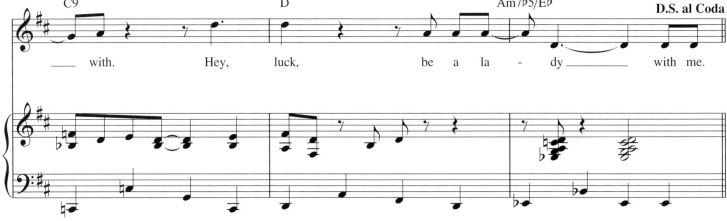

Stick with me, ba - by, I'm ___ the fel - la you ___ came in

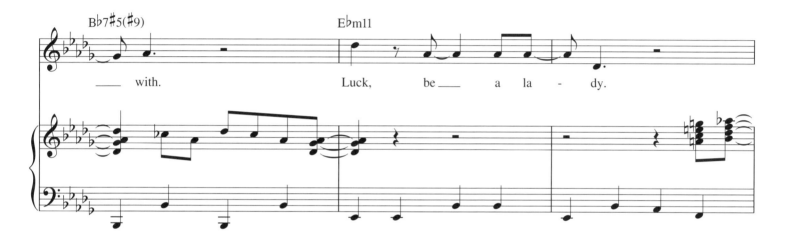

___ with. Luck, be ___ a la - dy.

Luck, be ___ a la -

- dy.

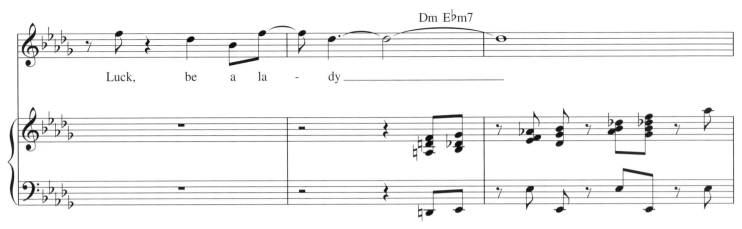

Luck, be a la - dy _____

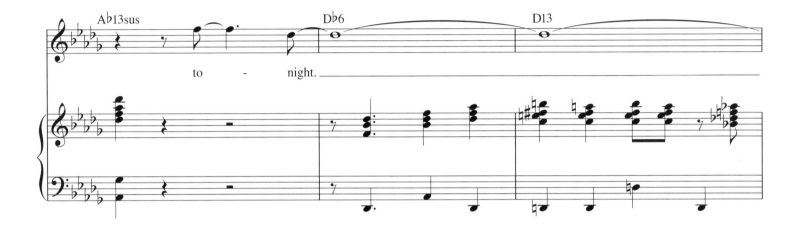

to - night. _____

MOONLIGHT BECOMES YOU

from the Paramount Picture ROAD TO MOROCCO

Words by JOHNNY BURKE
Music by JAMES VAN HEUSEN

Moderately slow, expressively

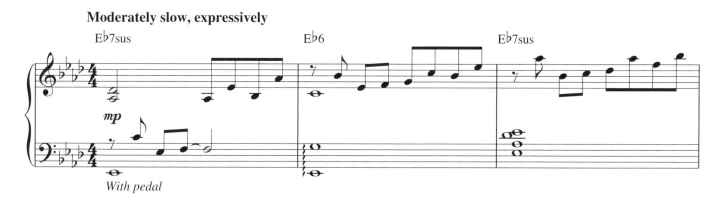

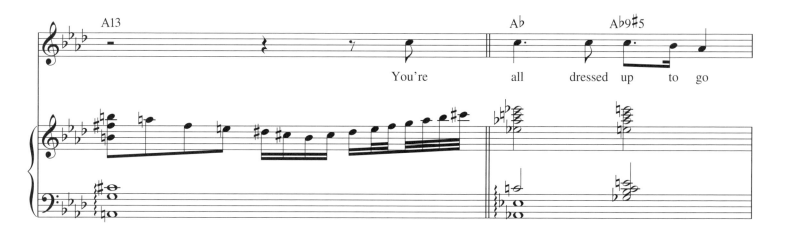

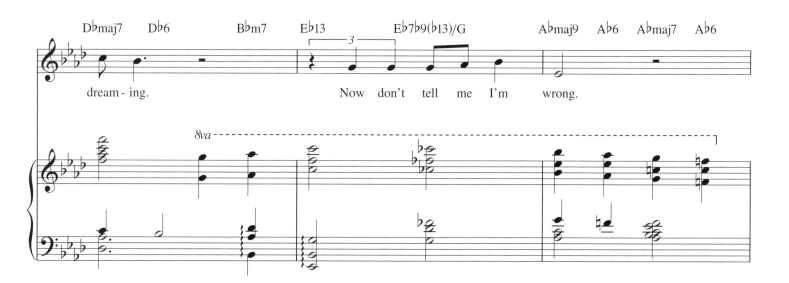

G7♭9(♯5)   A♭/C   Cm   Gm/D   Cm/E♭   B♭/F

And what a night____ to go dream-ing;

F7   Fm7/B♭   Gm/B♭   B♭7sus

mind____ if I tag a - long?

Moderately slow, steady Ballad

E♭   Edim   Fm7   B♭9♯11 B♭7♭9(♯11)   E♭6/9   Gm7   C♭7/G♭

Moon - light be - comes you. It goes with your

Fm7   B♭13   A♭m7   Gm7   C7♯11   C7   Fm7   B♭9

hair.____ You cer-tain-ly know the right thing to____

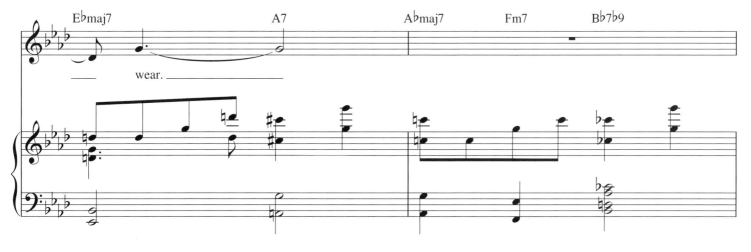

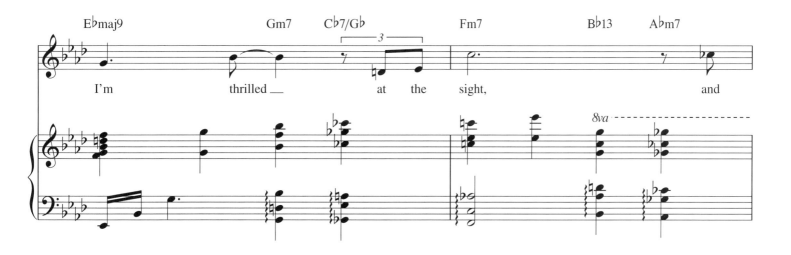

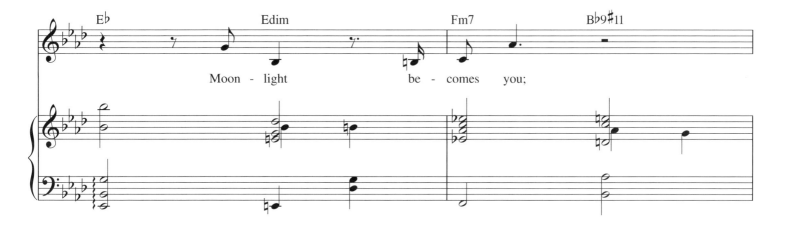

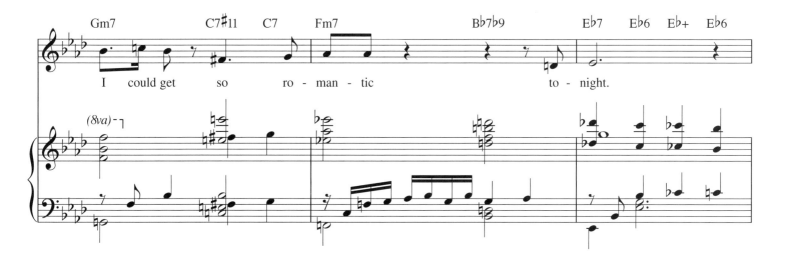

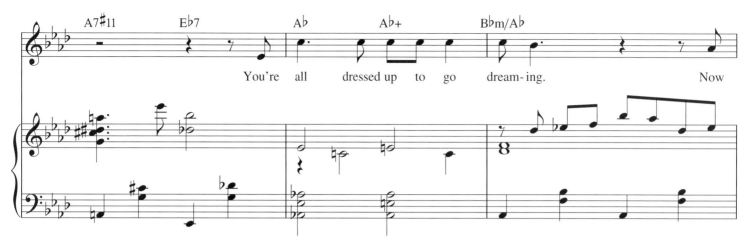

You're all dressed up to go dream-ing. Now

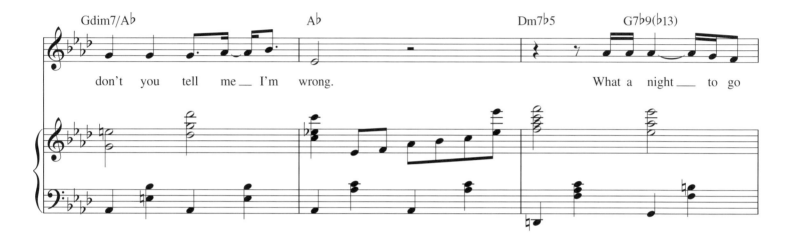

don't you tell me __ I'm wrong. What a night __ to go

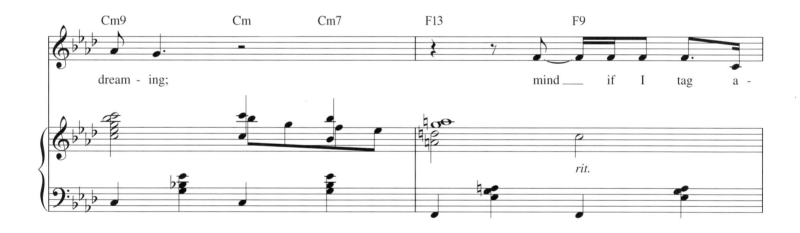

dream - ing; mind __ if I tag a -

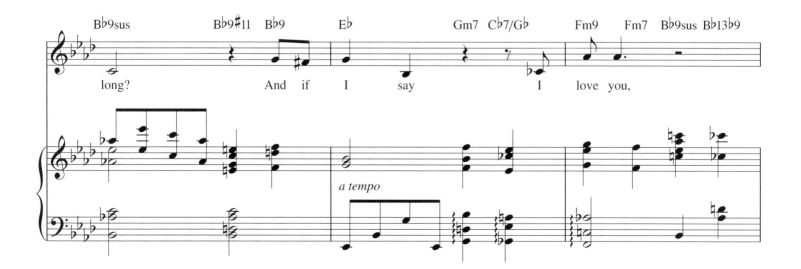

long? And if I say I love you,

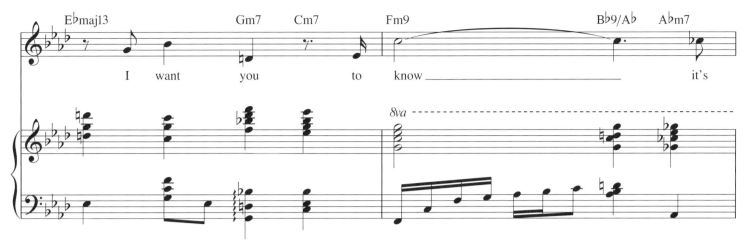

I want you to know _____ it's

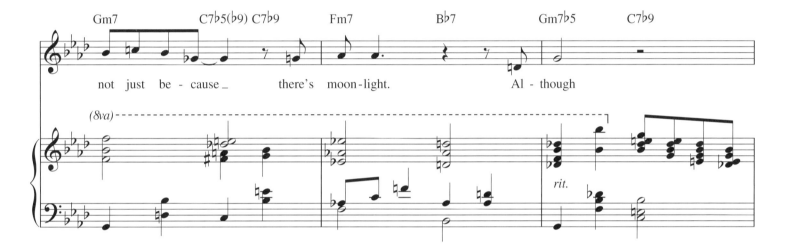

not just be - cause _ there's moon-light. Al - though

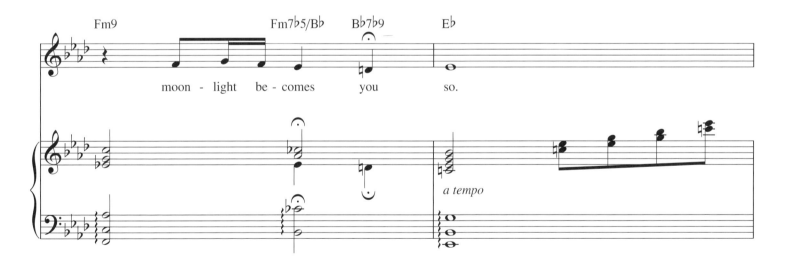

moon - light be - comes you so.

Very expressively

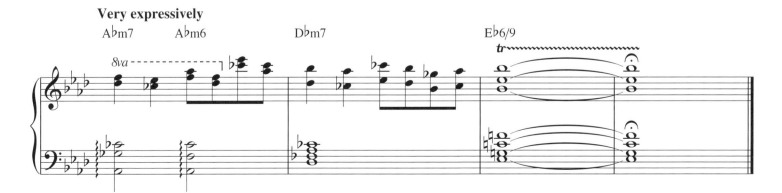

NICE WORK IF YOU CAN GET IT

from A DAMSEL IN DISTRESS

Music and Lyrics by GEORGE GERSHWIN
and IRA GERSHWIN

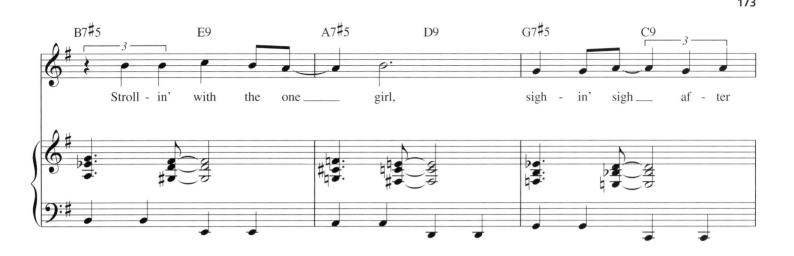

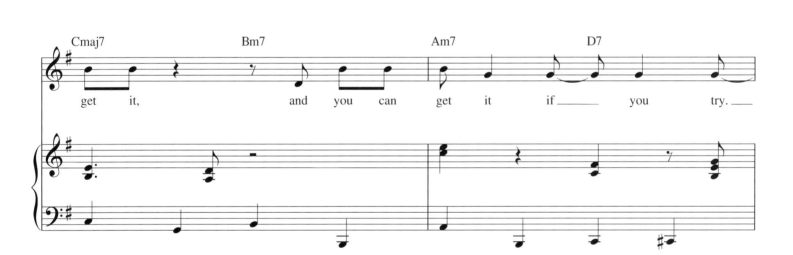

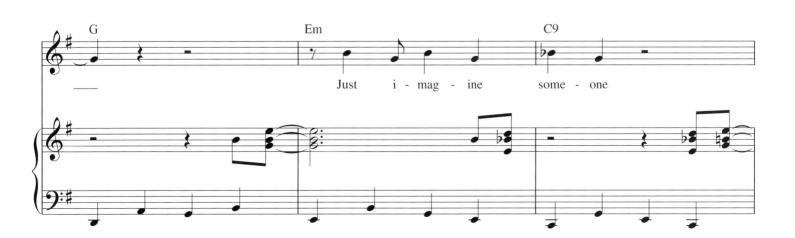

wait - in' at the cot-tage door, ___ where two ___ hearts be -

come one. Who could ask an - y - thing

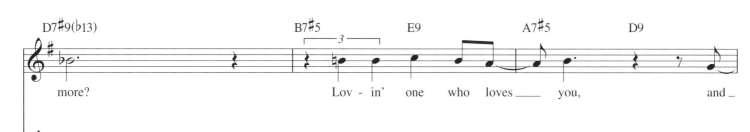

more? Lov - in' one who loves ___ you, and _

___ then tak - in' that vow. ___

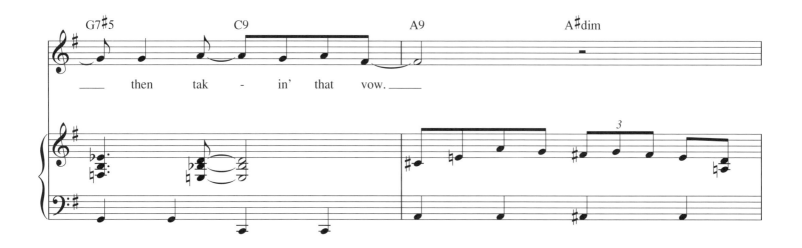

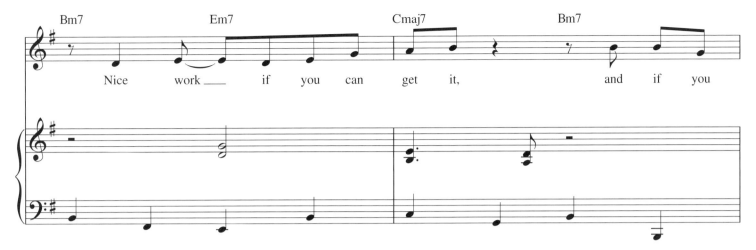

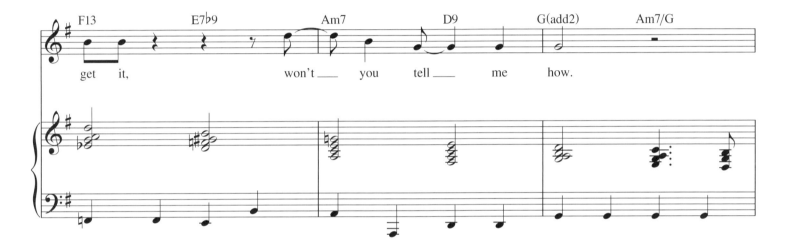

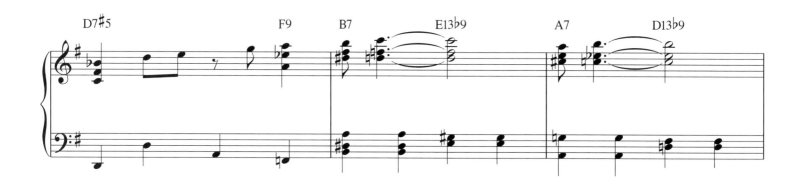

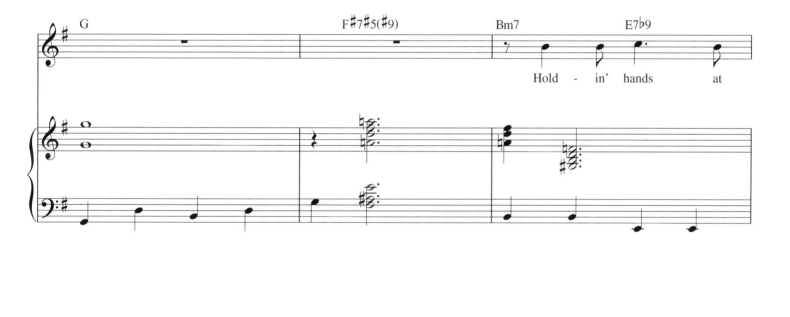

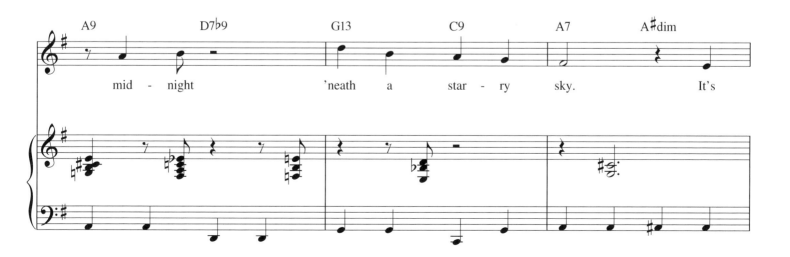

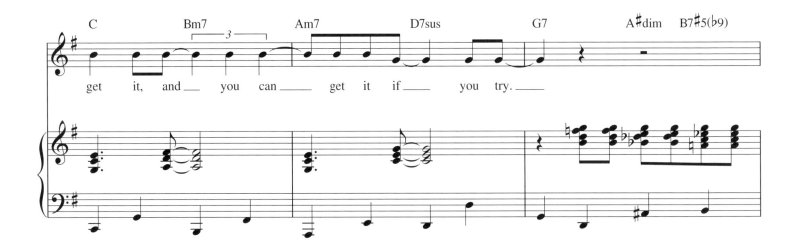

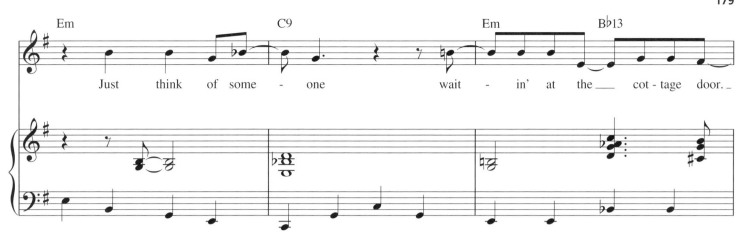

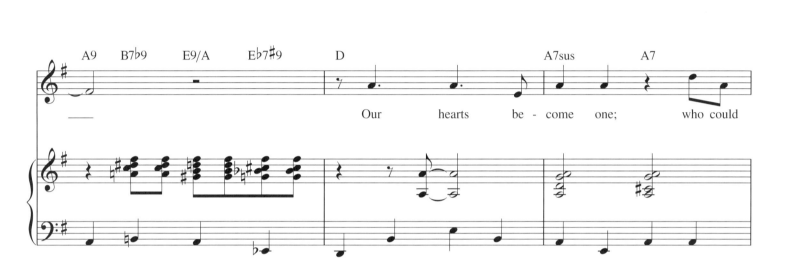

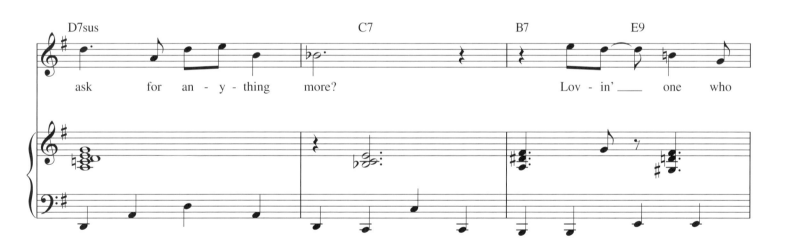

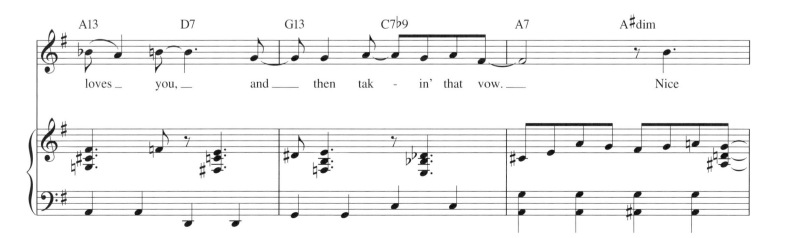

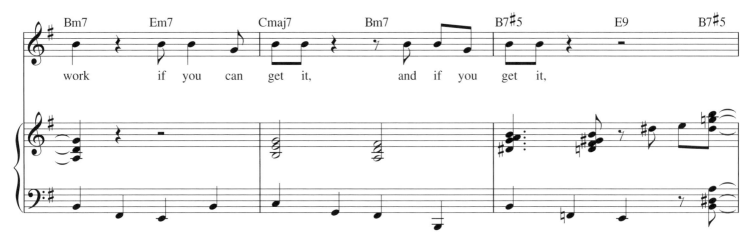

work if you can get it, and if you get it,

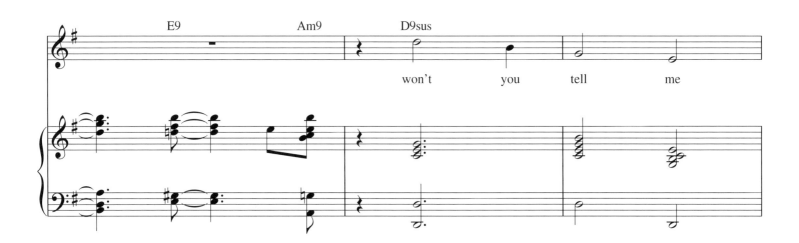

won't you tell me

how?

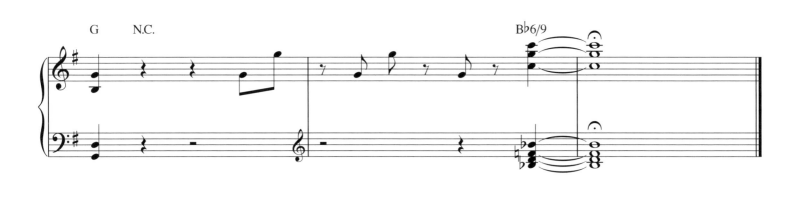

THE NIGHT WE CALLED IT A DAY

By TOM ADAIR
and MATT DENNIS

Slow Ballad

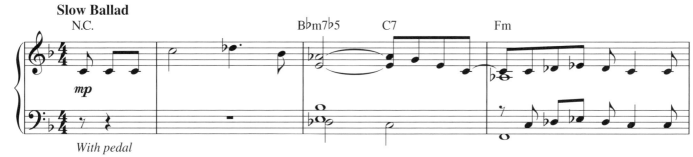

With pedal

There was a moon out in space, but a

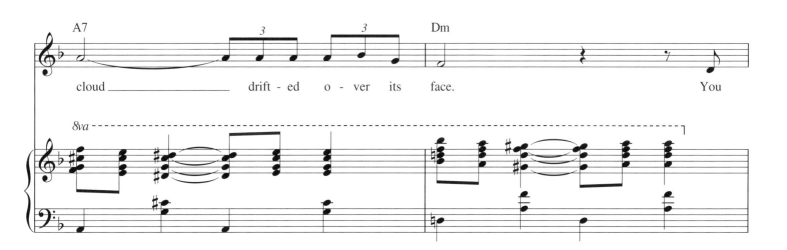

cloud _____ drift-ed o-ver its face. You

kissed me and went on your way, the

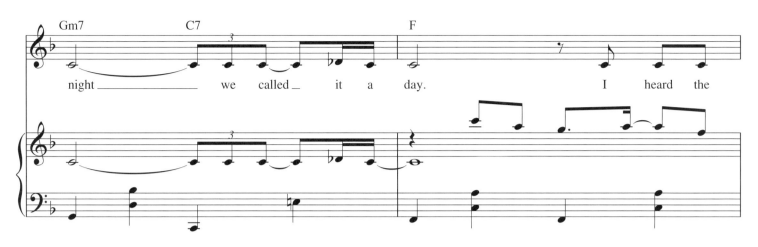

night _____ we called __ it a day. I heard the

song _____ of the spheres,

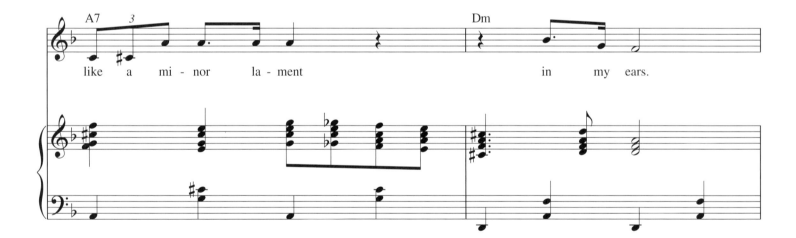

like a mi - nor la - ment in my ears.

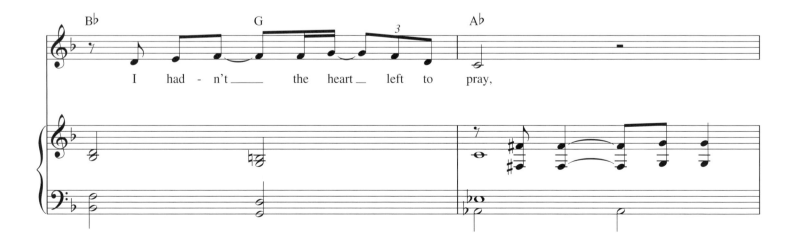

I had - n't _____ the heart _ left to pray,

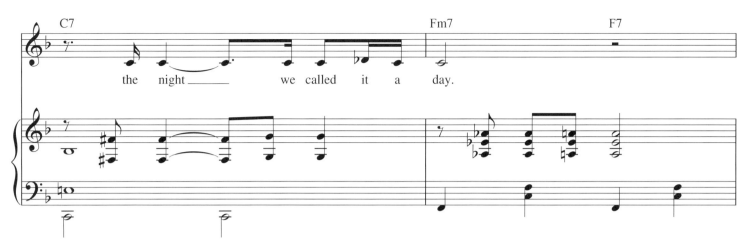

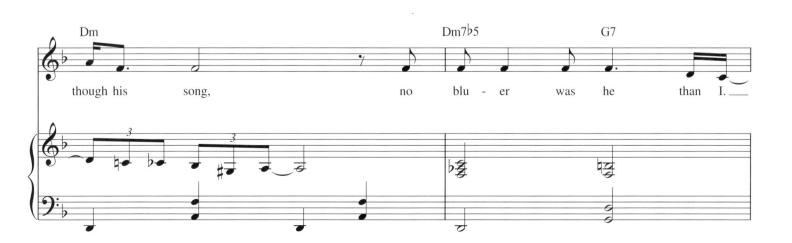

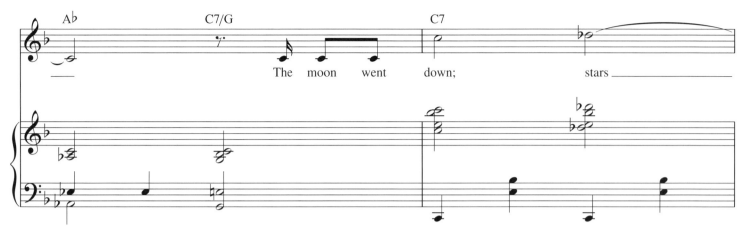

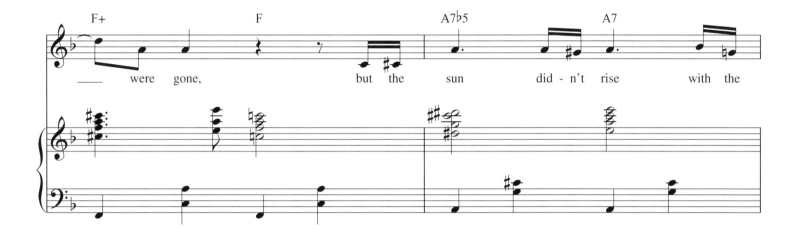

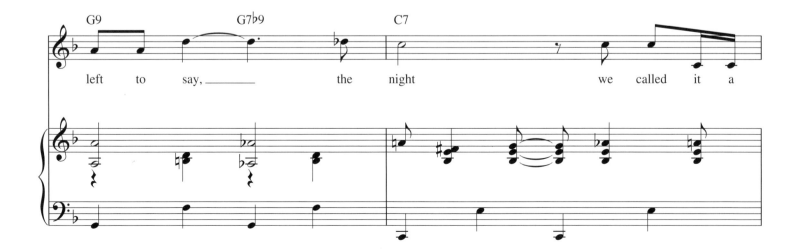

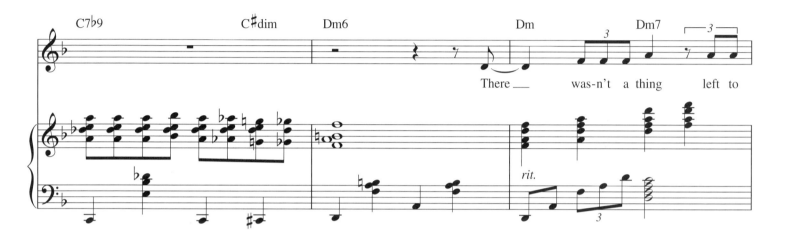

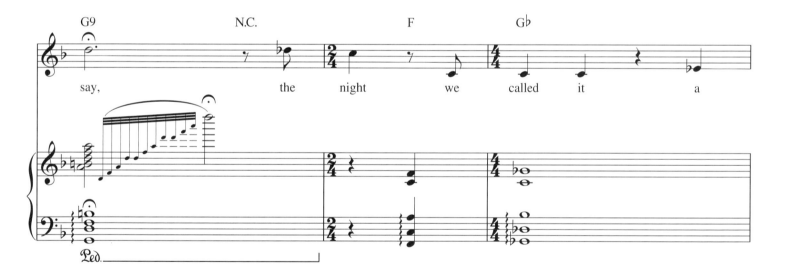

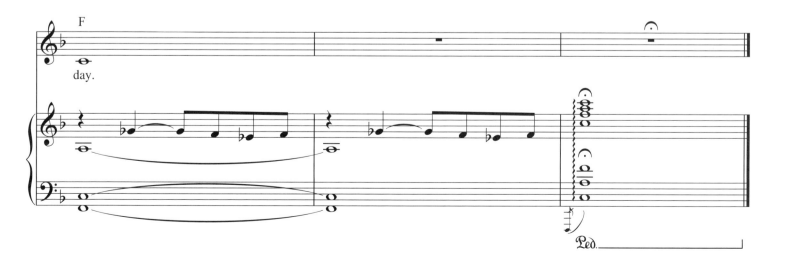

OLD DEVIL MOON

Words by E.Y. "YIP" HARBURG
Music by BURTON LANE

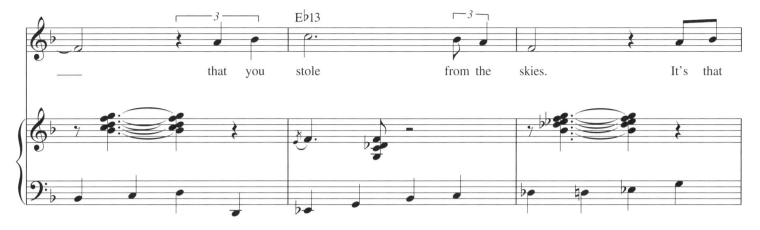

that you stole from the skies. It's that

old _____ dev - il moon _____ in your eyes.

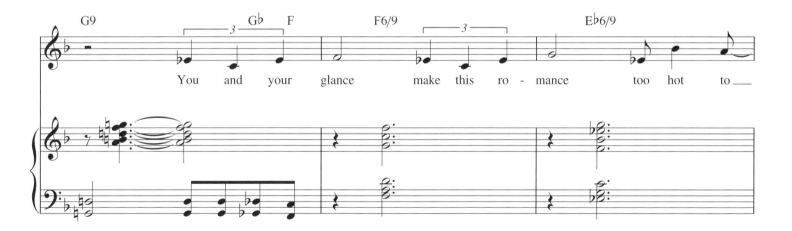

You and your glance make this ro - mance too hot to ___

___ han - dle. Stars in the night, ___ blaz - ing their

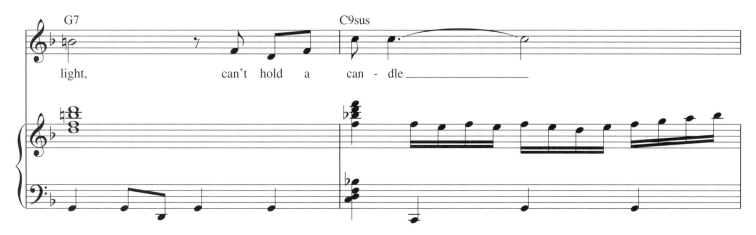

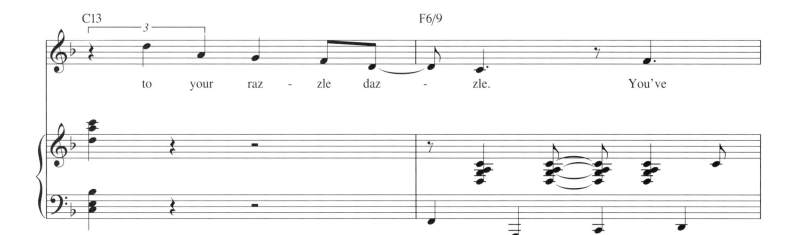

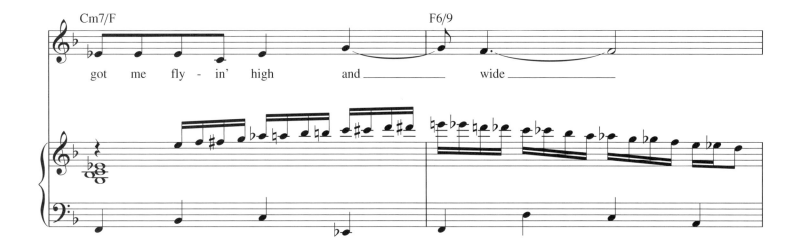

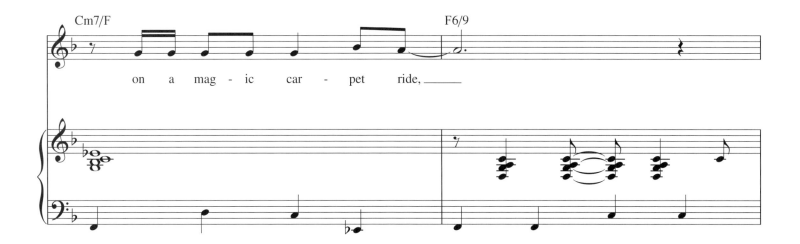

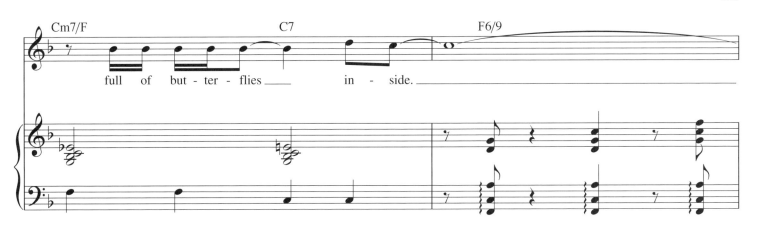

full of but - ter - flies _____ in - side. _____

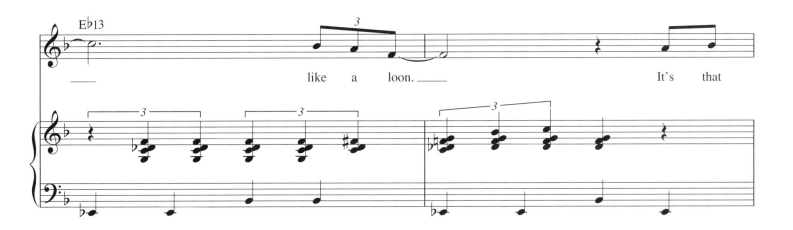

_____ Wan-na cry, wan - na croon, _____ wan-na laugh _

_____ like a loon. _____ It's that

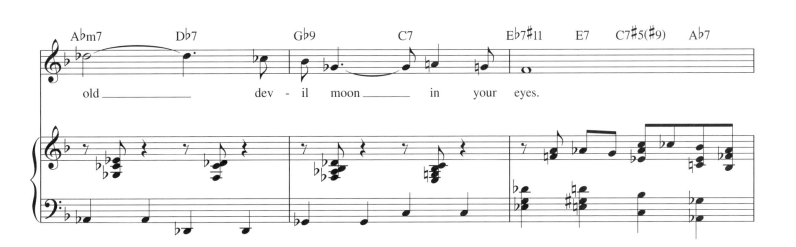

old _____ dev - il moon _____ in your eyes.

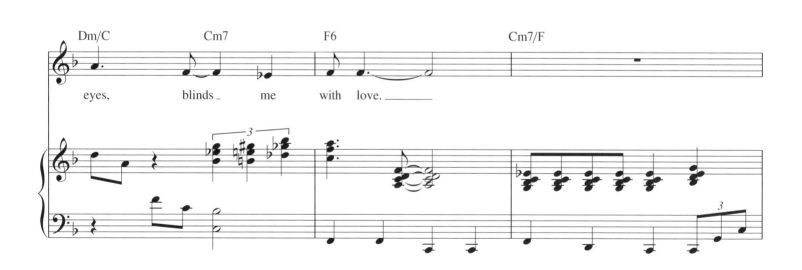

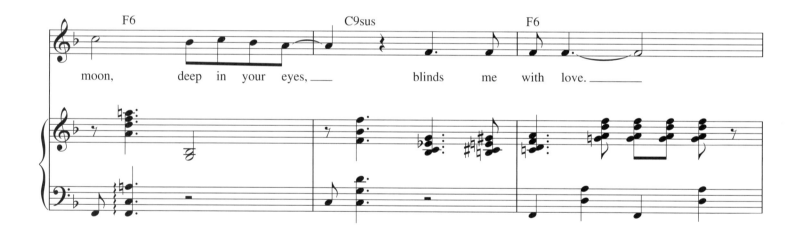

ONLY THE LONELY

Words by SAMMY CAHN
Music by JAMES VAN HEUSEN

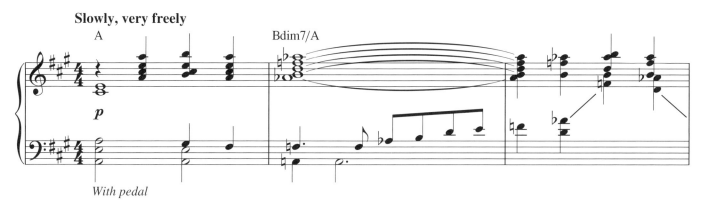

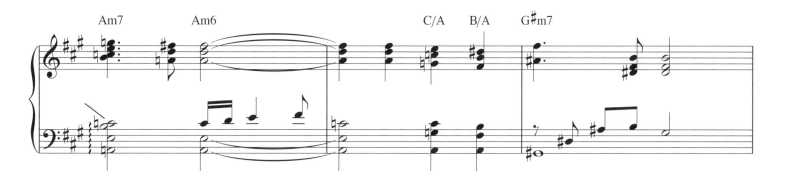

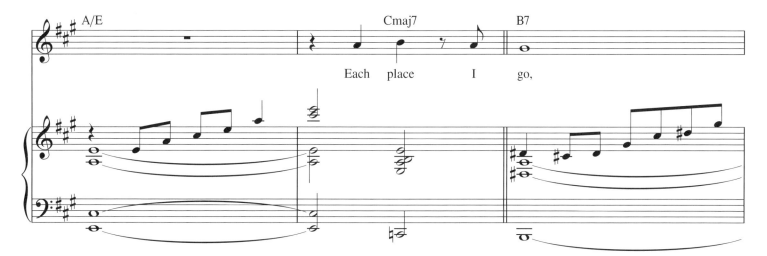

Each place I go,

194

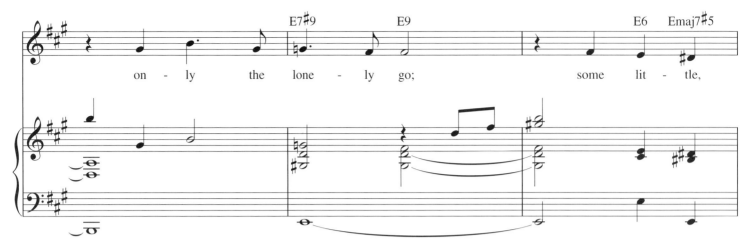

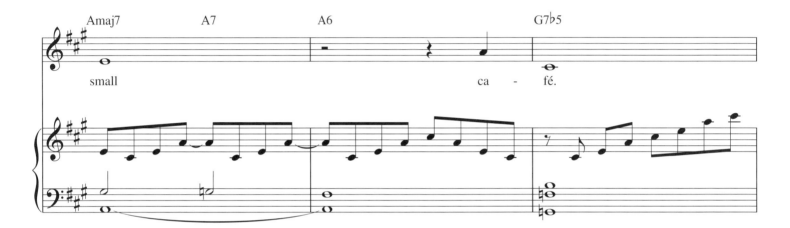

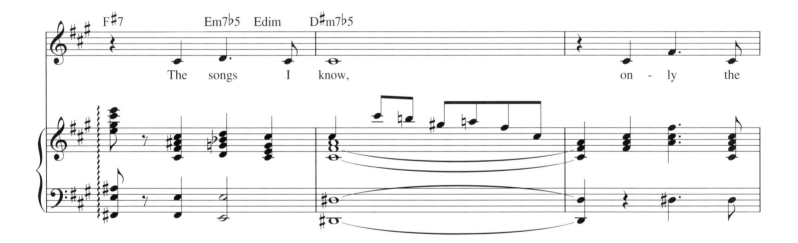

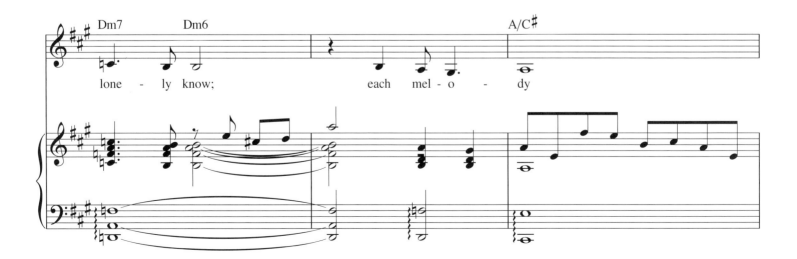

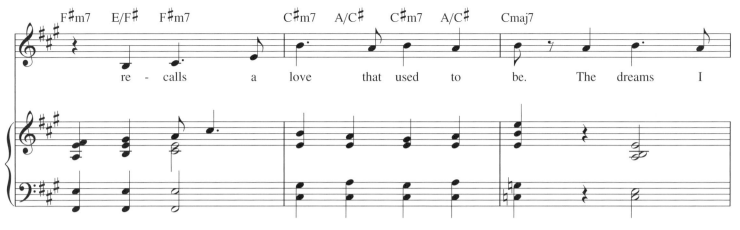

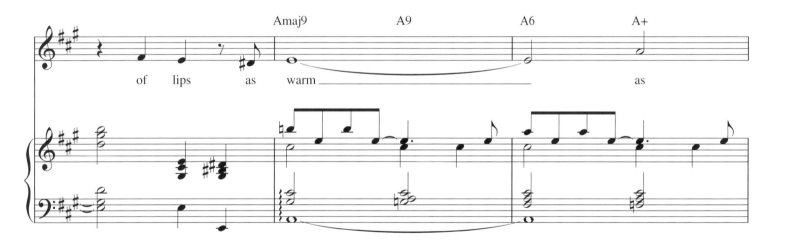

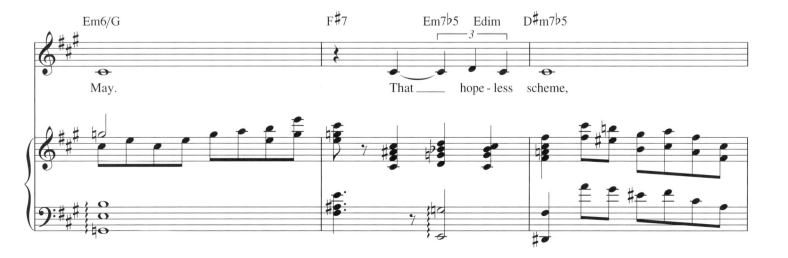

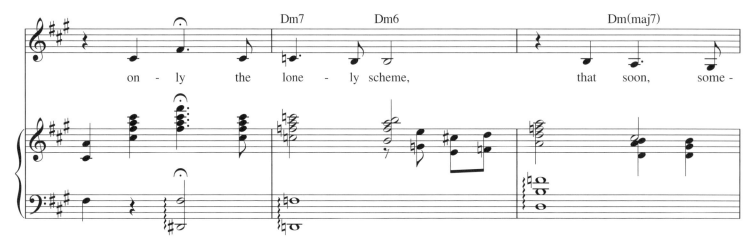

on - ly the lone - ly scheme, that soon, some -

where, you'll find the one that used to

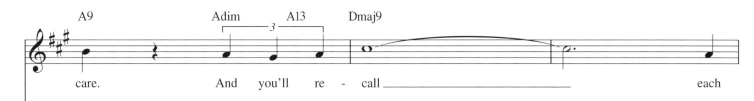

care. And you'll re - call _____ each

fun time, those pic - nics at the

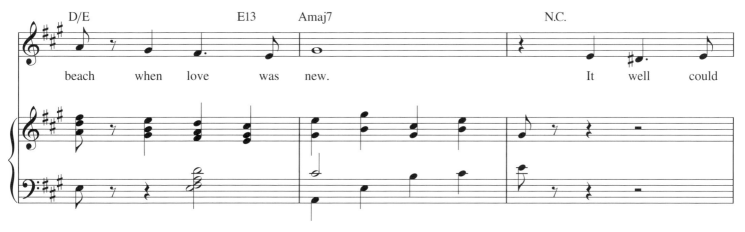

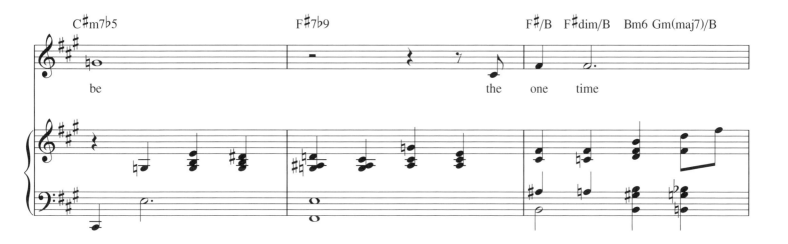

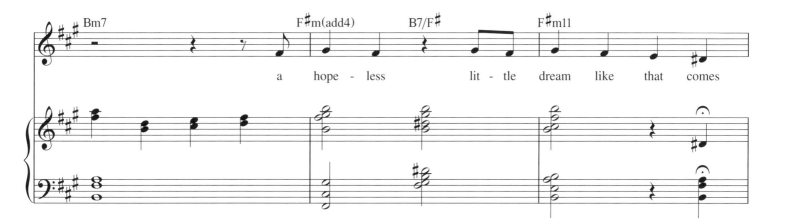

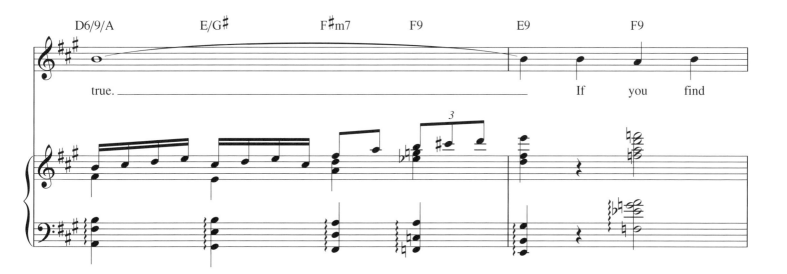

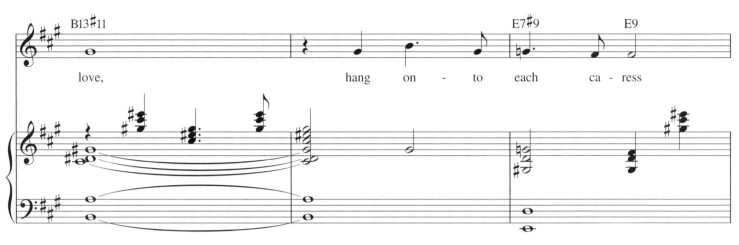

love,   hang on - to each ca - ress

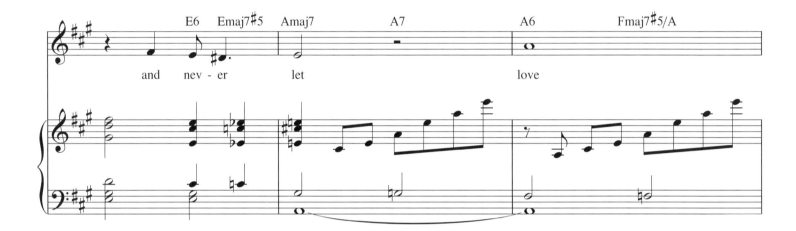

and nev - er   let   love

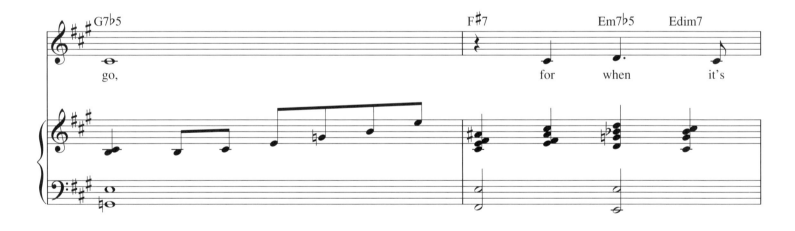

go,   for when   it's

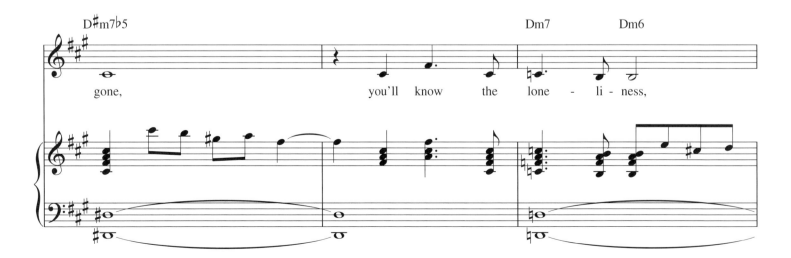

gone,   you'll know   the   lone - li - ness,

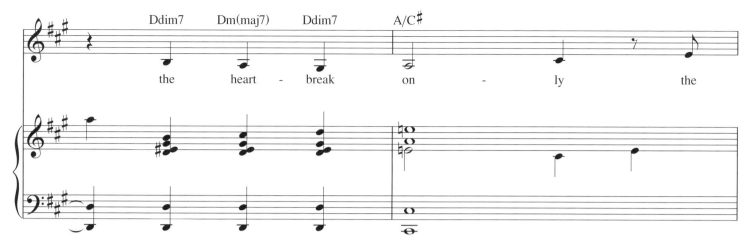

the heart - break on - ly the

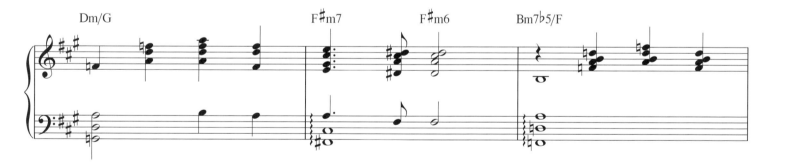

lone - ly know.

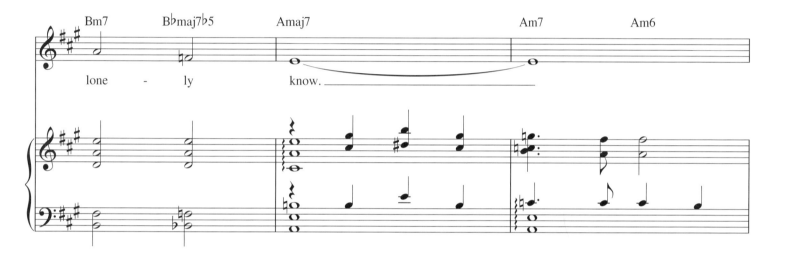

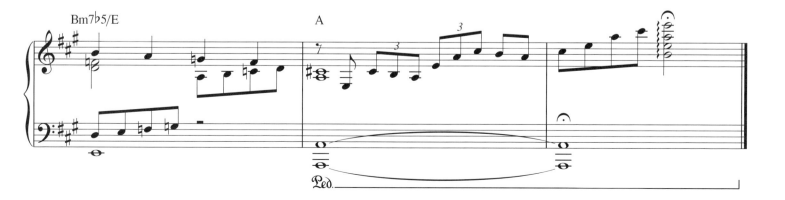

Ped.

POCKETFUL OF MIRACLES

Words by SAMMY CAHN
Music by JAMES VAN HEUSEN

Moderate 2-beat

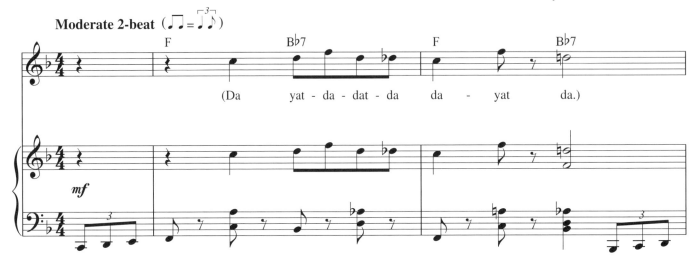

(Da yat - da - dat - da da - yat da.)

(Da dat - da - dat - da da - yat da.)

Pee - rac - ti - cal - i - ty
Tee - rou - bles more or less

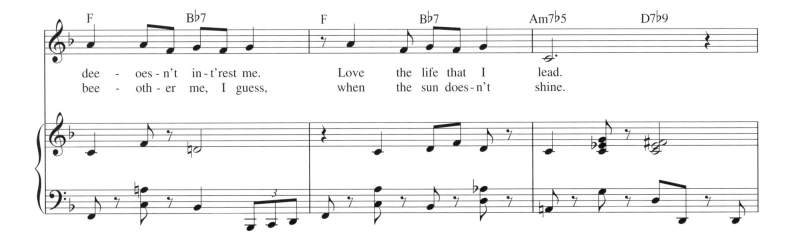

dee - oes - n't in - t'rest me. Love the life that I lead.
bee - oth - er me, I guess, when the sun does - n't shine.

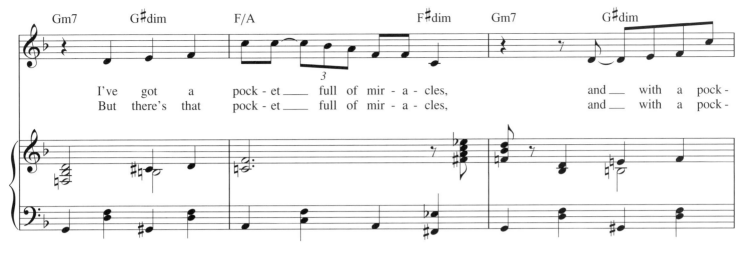

I've got a pock - et ___ full of mir - a - cles, and ___ with a pock -
But there's that pock - et ___ full of mir - a - cles, and ___ with a pock -

et full of mir - a - cles, one ___ lit - tle mir -
et full of mir - a - cles, the ___ world's a bright

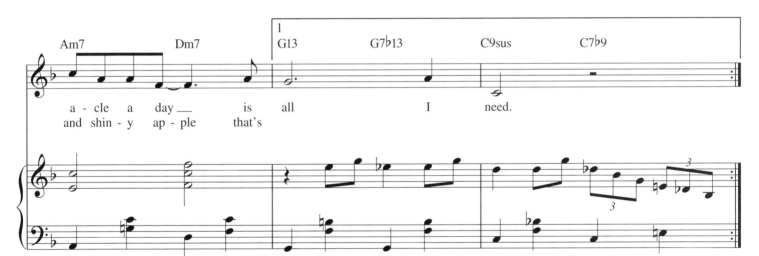

a - cle a day ___ is all I need.
and shin - y ap - ple that's

mine, all mine. I hear

down and out of mir - a - cles,   I've got a   pock - et full of mir - a - cles,

and there'll be   mir - a - cles e - nough   for   you

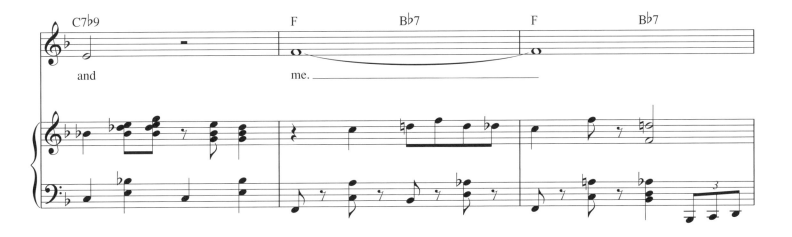

and   me. _____

D.S. al Coda

CODA

free.

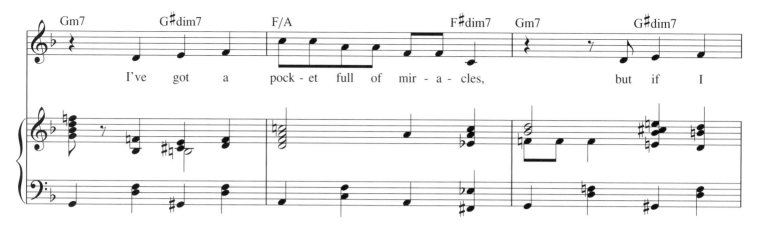

I've got a pock-et full of mir-a-cles, but if I

had to pick a mir-a-cle, my fav-'rite mir-a-cle of all is

you and me. _____

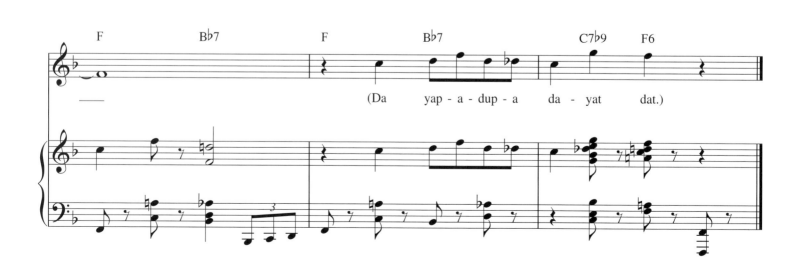

____ (Da yap-a-dup-a da-yat dat.)

RIVER, STAY 'WAY FROM MY DOOR

Written by MORT DIXON
and HARRY WOODS

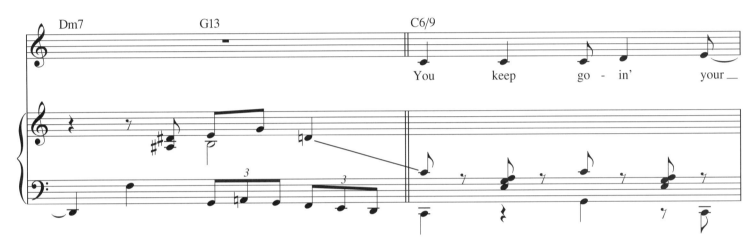

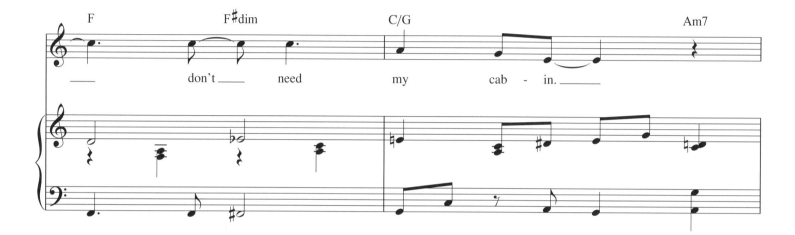

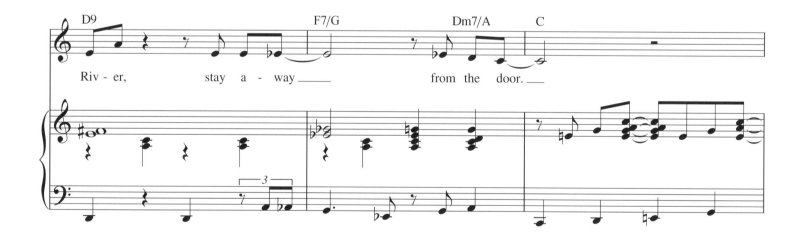

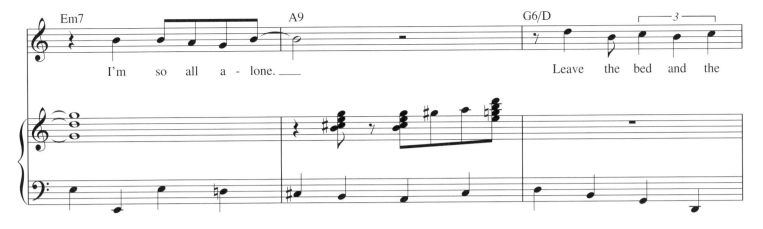

I'm so all a - lone. ___ Leave the bed and the

fire; ___ that is all ___ I own. ___

I ain't break-ing your heart; don't start ___ break - ing

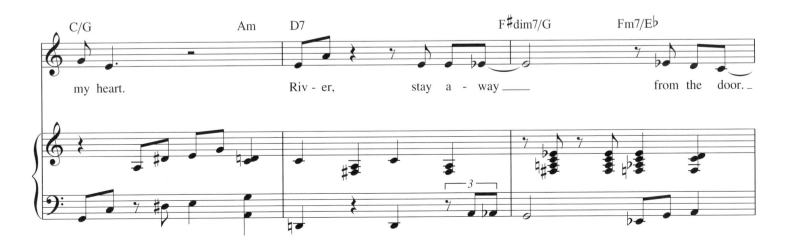

my heart. Riv - er, stay a - way ___ from the door. ___

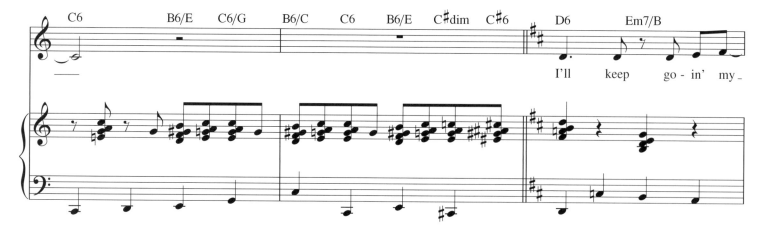

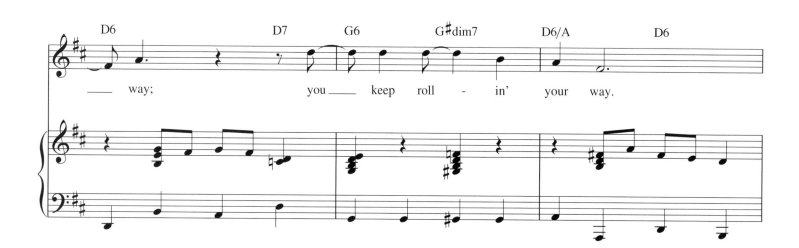

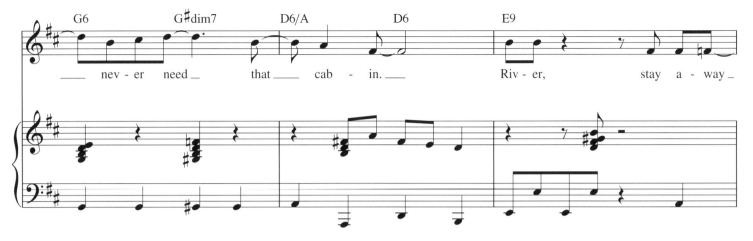

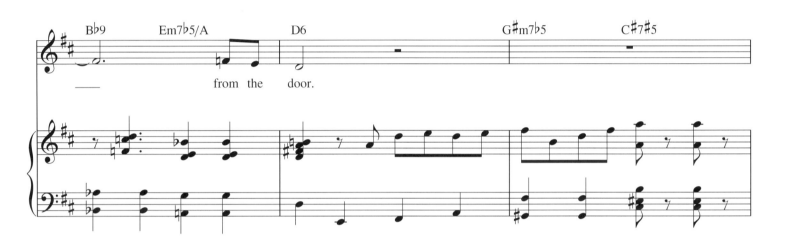

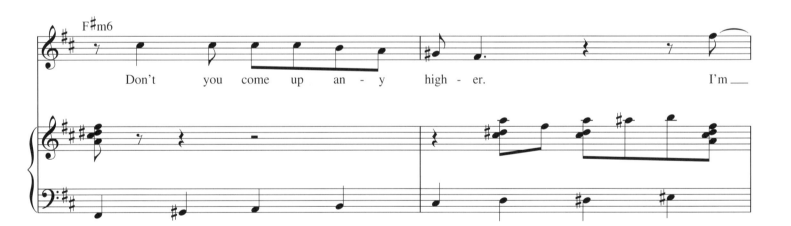

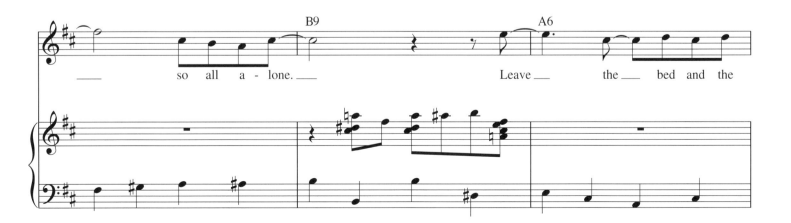

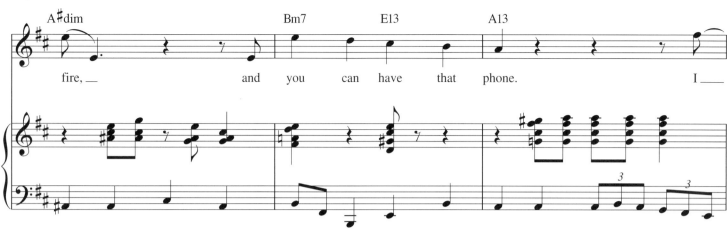

fire, ___ and you can have that phone. I ___

___ ain't break - in' your heart; ___ don't you start ___ break - in'

my heart. Riv - er, stay a - way ___ from the

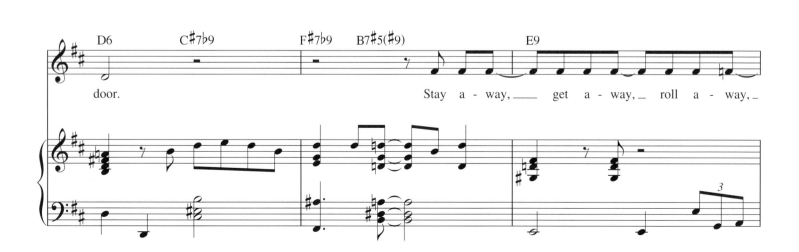

door. Stay a - way, ___ get a - way, ___ roll a - way, ___

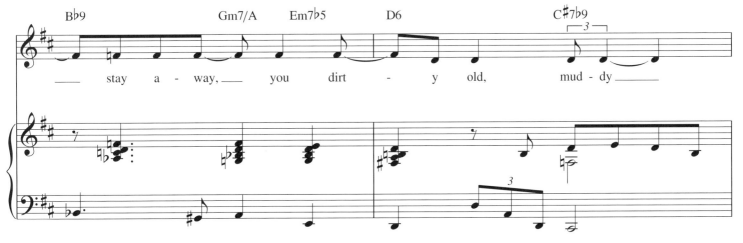

stay a - way, ___ you dirt - y old, mud - dy ___

riv - er, you. Riv - er, stay a - way ___

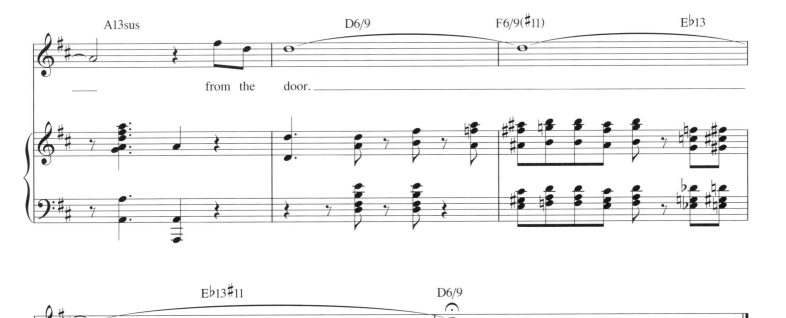

___ from the door. ___

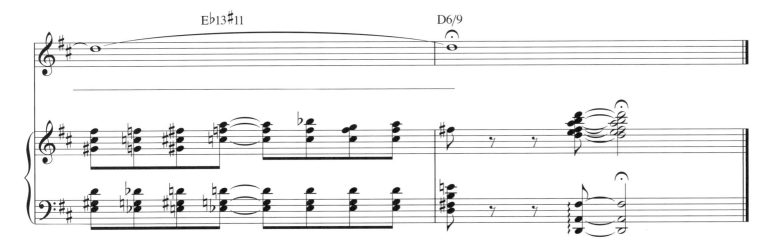

SATURDAY NIGHT
(Is the Loneliest Night of the Week)

Words by SAMMY CAHN
Music by JULE STYNE

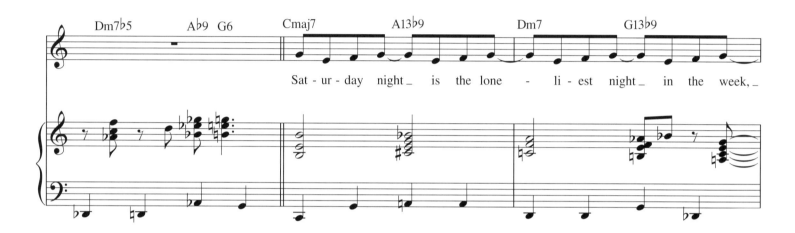

Sat - ur - day night _ is the lone - li - est night _ in the week,

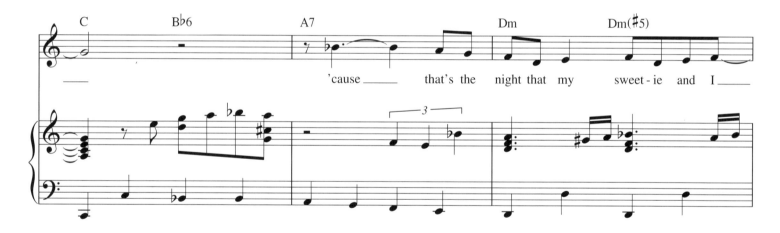

___ 'cause ___ that's the night that my sweet - ie and I ___

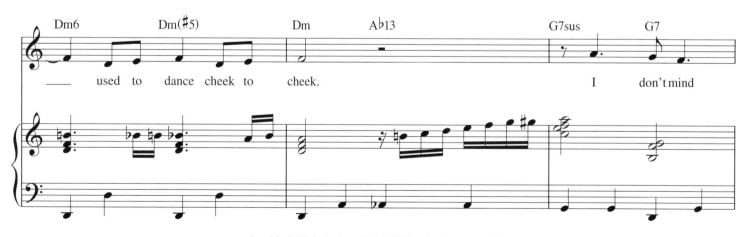

___ used to dance cheek to cheek. I don't mind

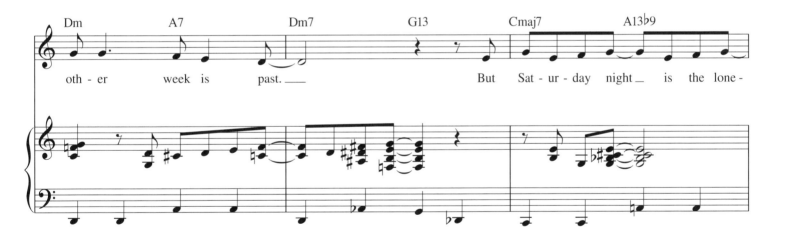

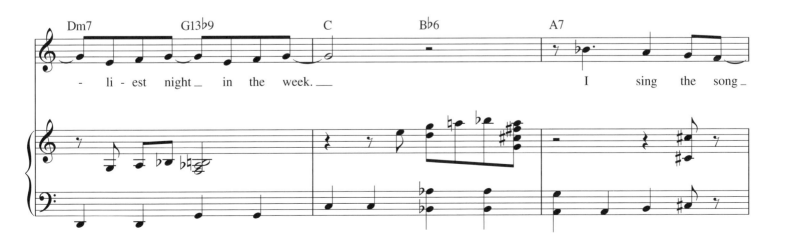

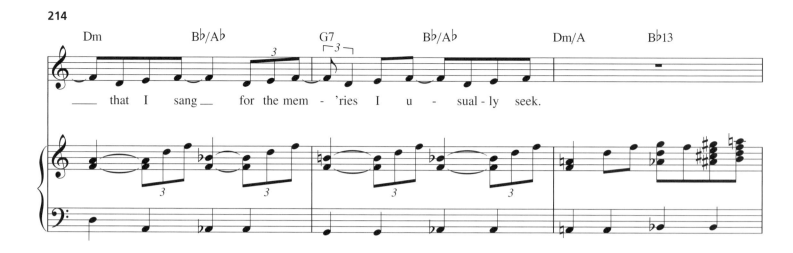

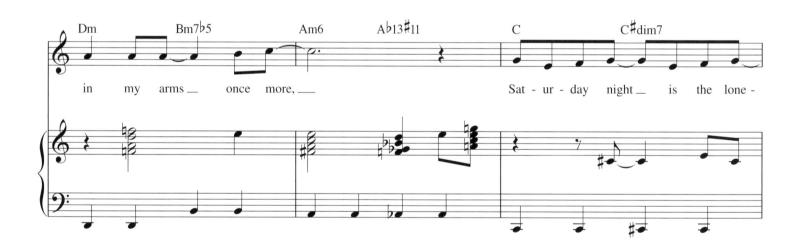

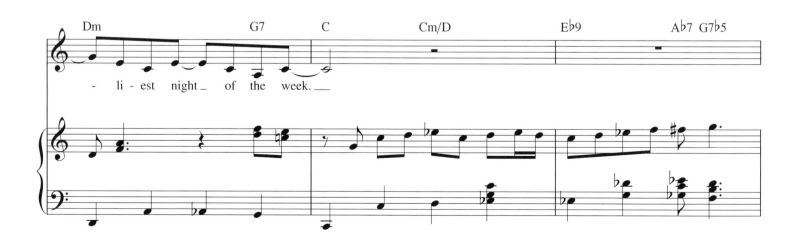

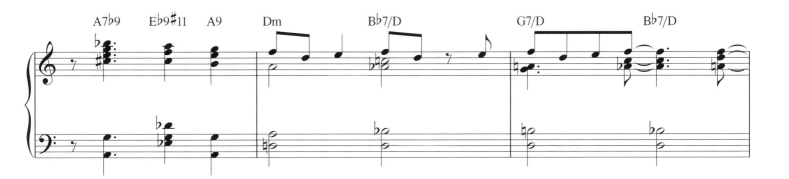

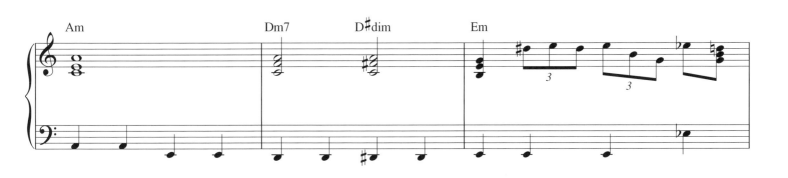

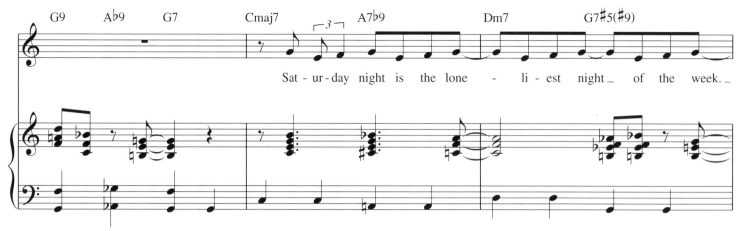

Sat - ur - day night is the lone - li - est night of the week.

I sing the song that I sang for the mem -

'ries I u - sual - ly seek. Un - til I

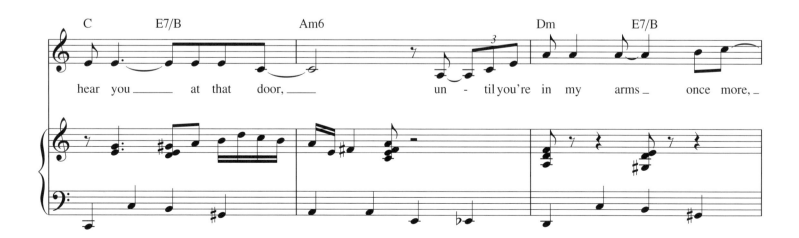

hear you at that door, un - til you're in my arms once more,

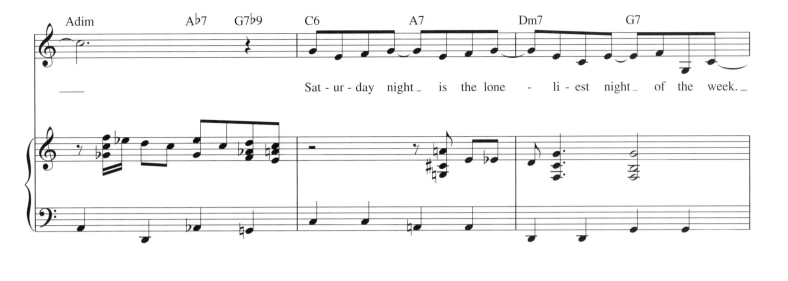

Sat - ur - day night _ is the lone - li - est night _ of the week. _

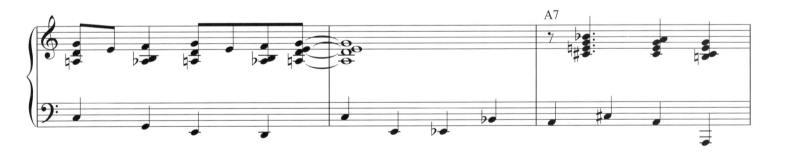

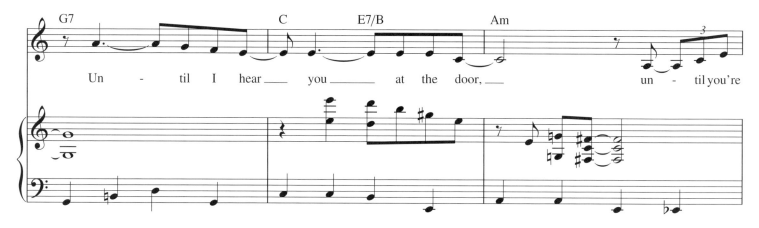

Un - til I hear ___ you ___ at the door, ___ un - til you're

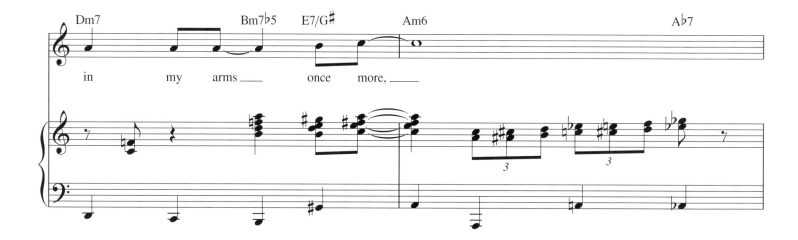

in my arms ___ once more, ___

Sat - ur - day night ___ is the lone - li - est night ___ of the week. ___

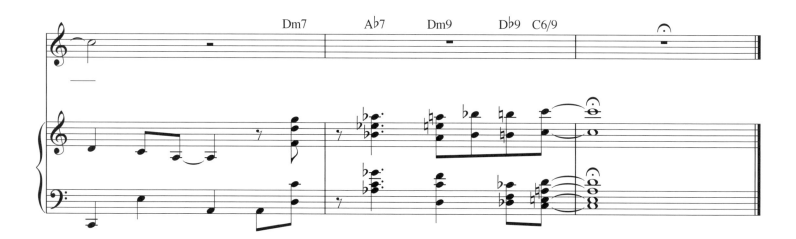

SLEEP WARM

Words and Music by ALAN BERGMAN,
LEW SPENCE and MARILYN KEITH

Sleep warm, sleep tight

when you ___ turn off the light. Sleep warm, sleep

well, my love. Rest your head

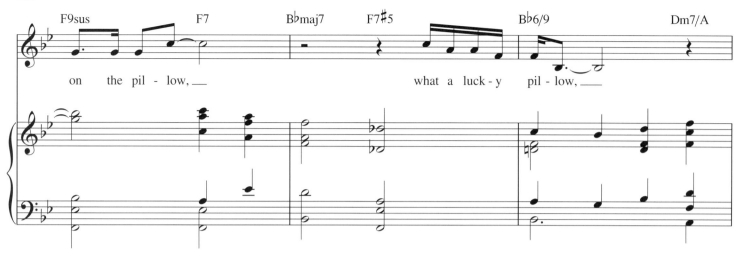

on the pil-low, ___ what a luck-y pil-low, ___

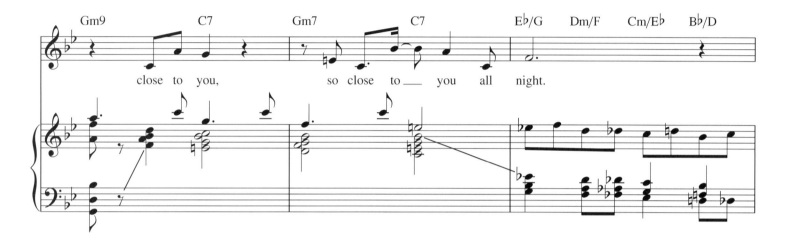

close to you, so close to ___ you all night.

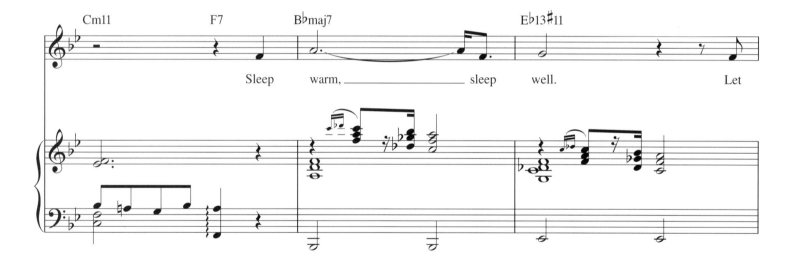

Sleep warm, _____ sleep well. Let

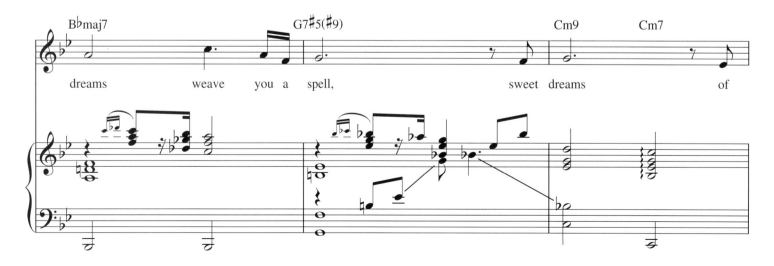

dreams weave you a spell, sweet dreams of

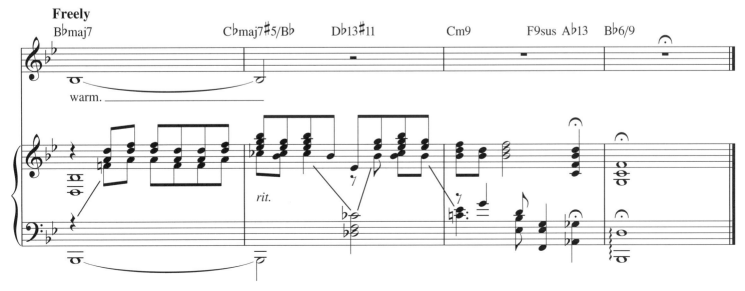

SEND IN THE CLOWNS

from the Musical A LITTLE NIGHT MUSIC
As recorded "Live at Madison Square Garden"

Words and Music by
STEPHEN SONDHEIM

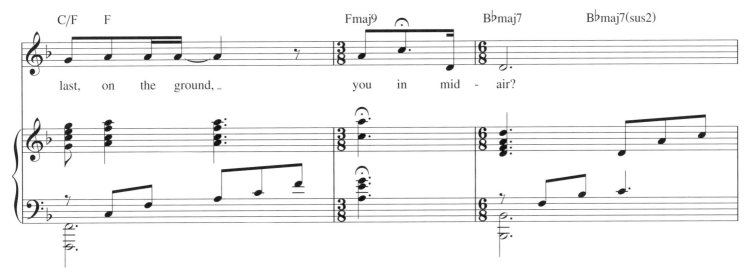

last, on the ground, __ you in mid - air?

Send in the clowns. Is - n't it

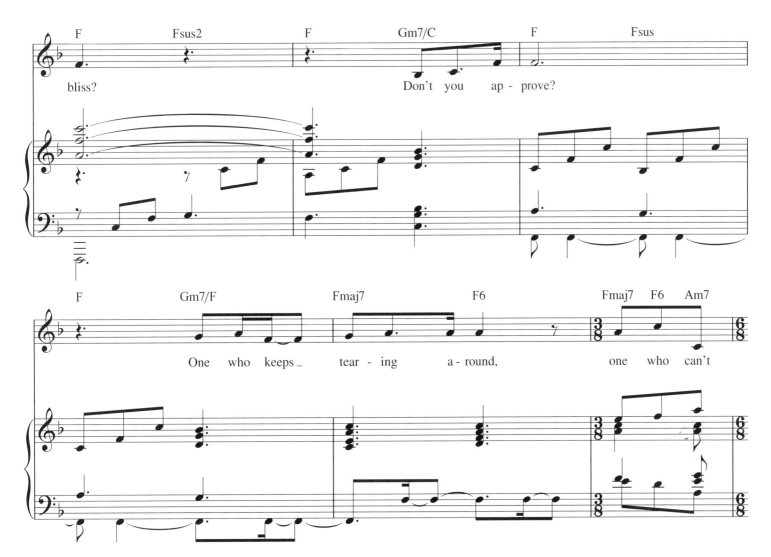

bliss? Don't you ap - prove?

One who keeps __ tear - ing a - round, one who can't

yours,   mak - ing   my   en - trance a - gain with my

a tempo

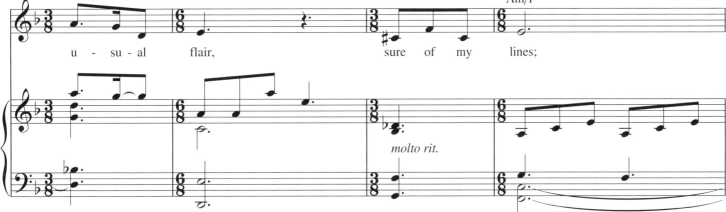

u - su - al   flair,   sure   of   my   lines;

molto rit.

Slowly, expressively

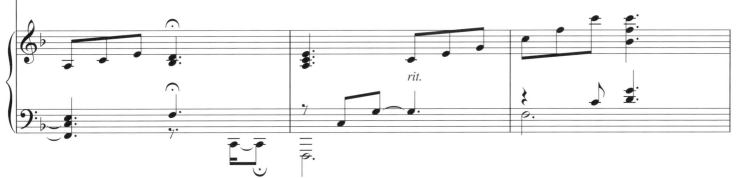

no - bod - y's   there.   Don't you love

rit.

farce?   My fault,   I   fear.

SOMEBODY LOVES ME

Words by B.G. DeSYLVA
and BALLARD MacDONALD
Music by GEORGE GERSHWIN
French Version by EMELIA RENAUD

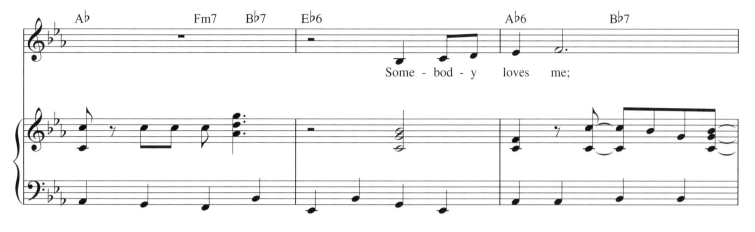

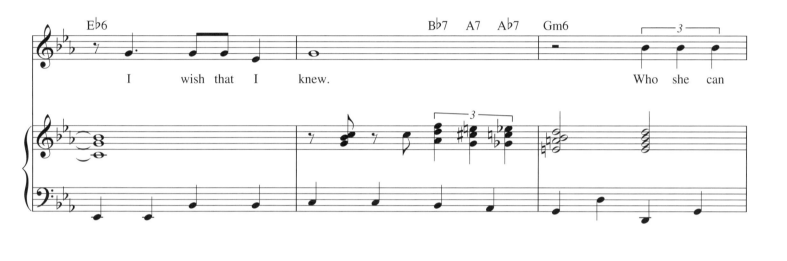

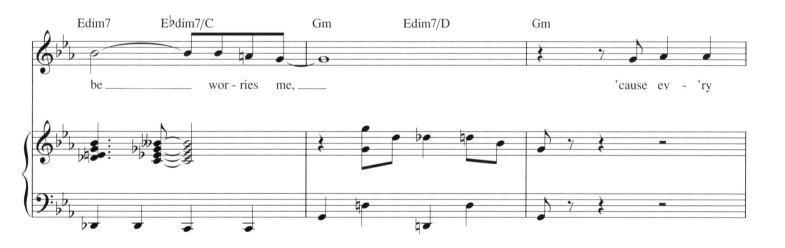

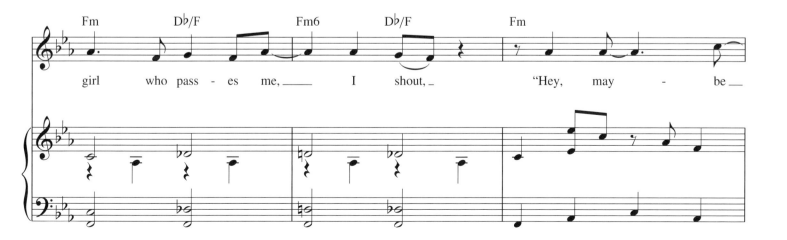

you were meant to be my ___ lov - in' ba -

- by." ___   Some - bod - y

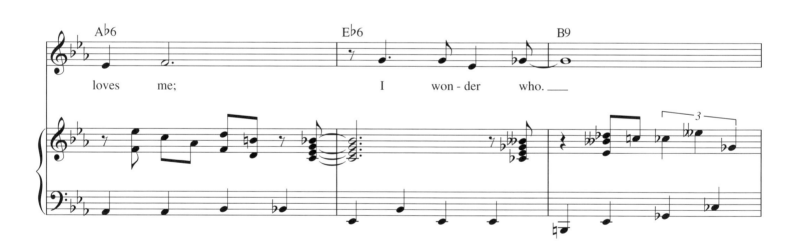

loves me;   I won - der who. ___

May - be ___   it's you. ___

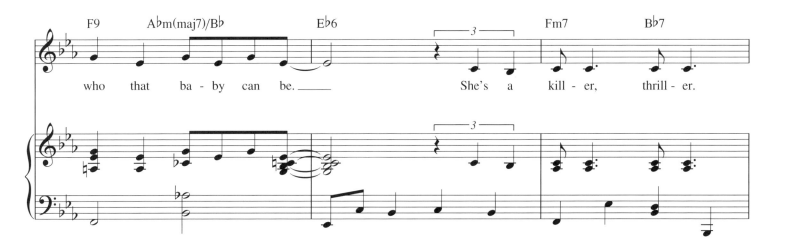

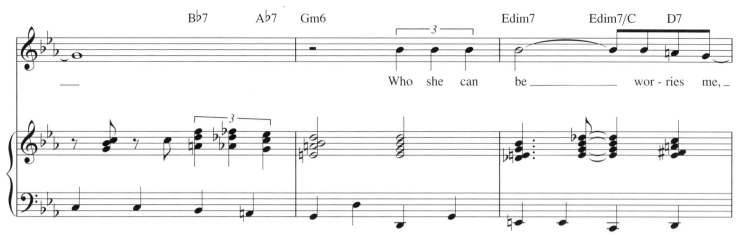

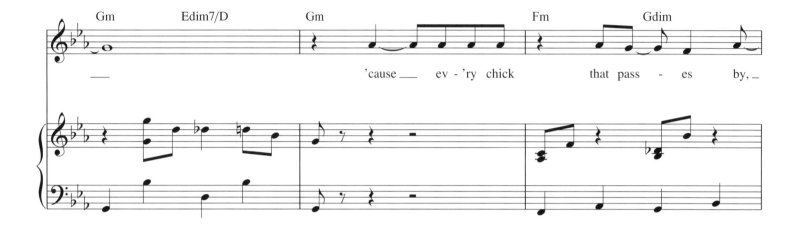

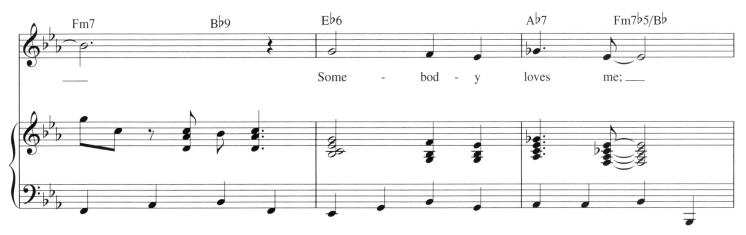

Some - bod - y loves me; ___

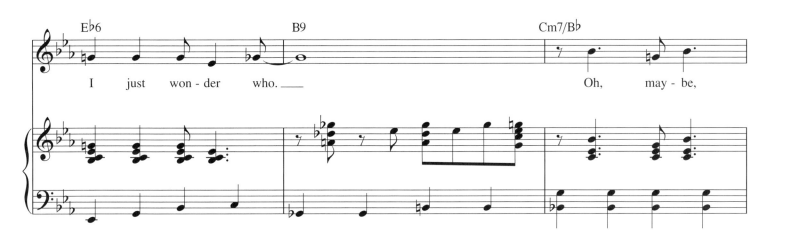

I just won - der who. ___ Oh, may - be,

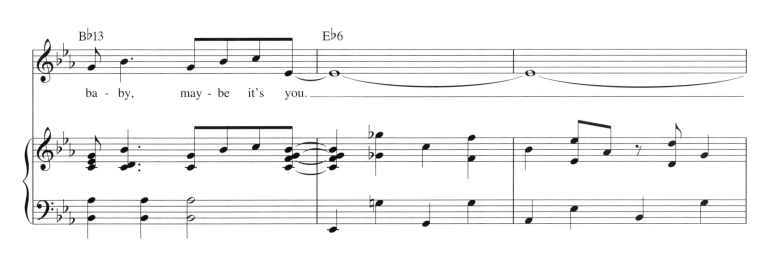

ba - by, may - be it's you. ___

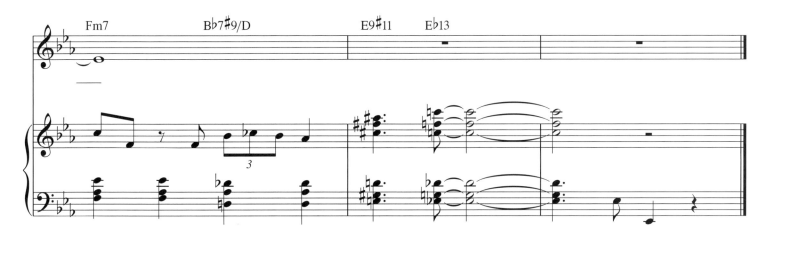

SWINGIN' DOWN THE LANE

Words by GUS KAHN
Music by ISHAM JONES

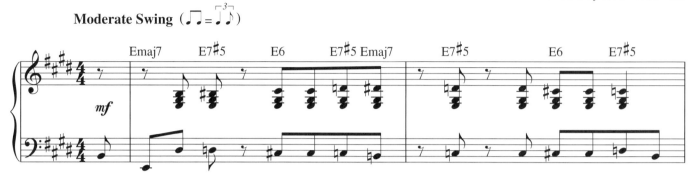

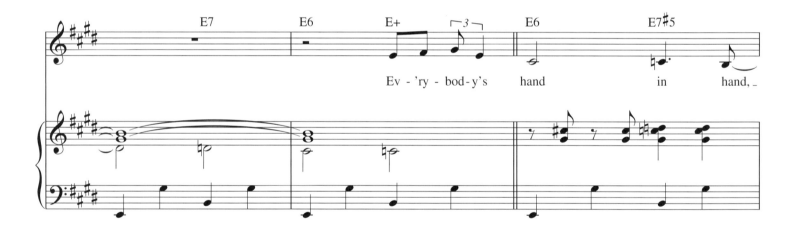

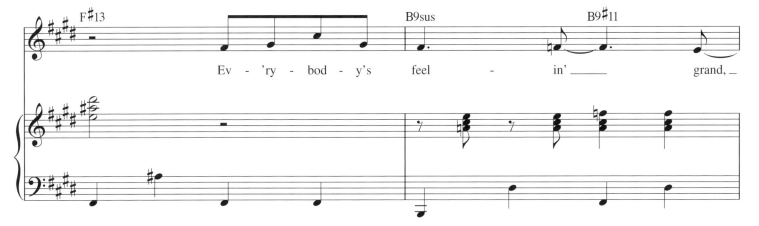

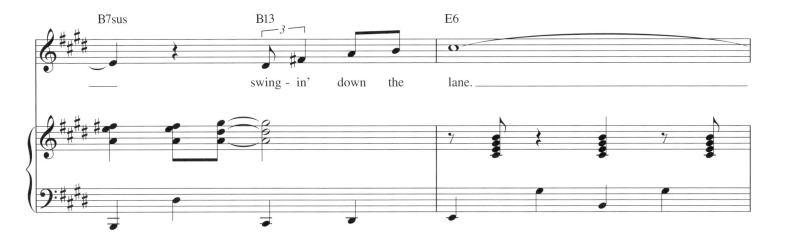

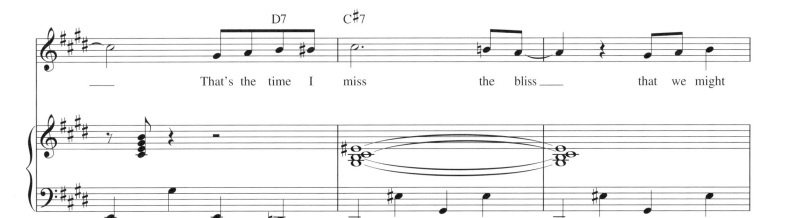

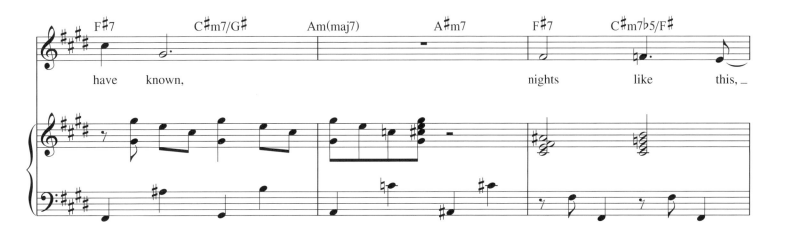

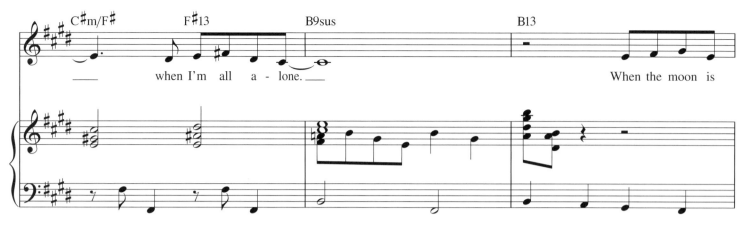

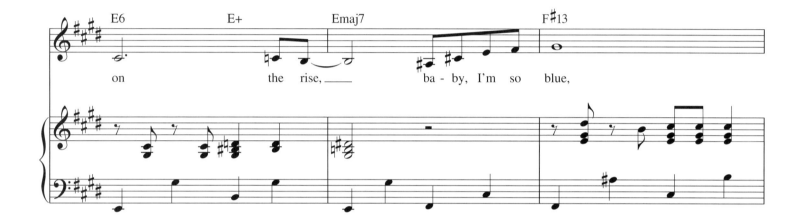

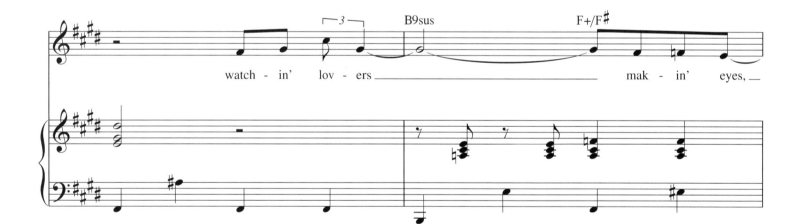

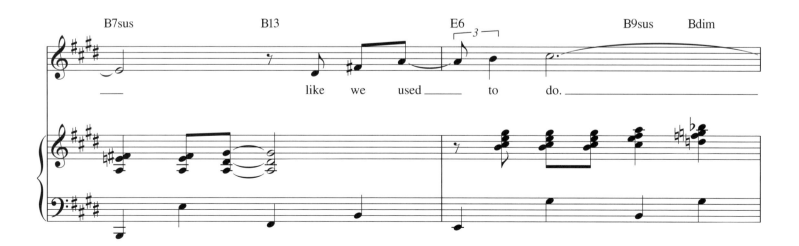

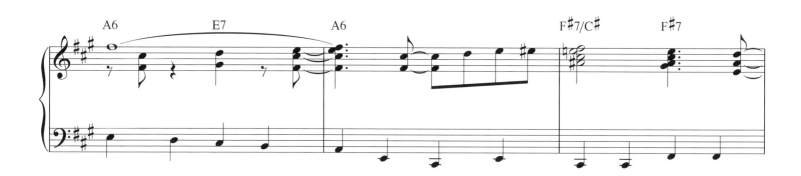

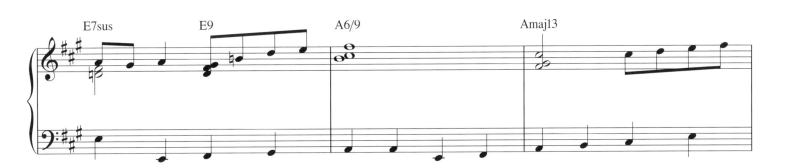

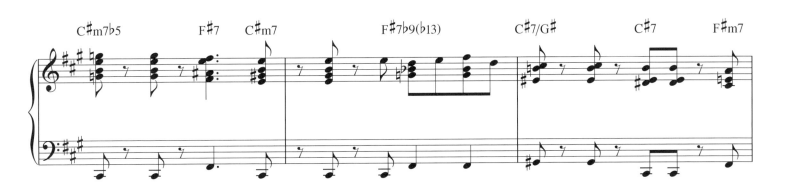

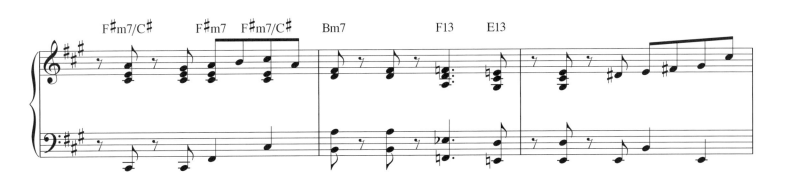

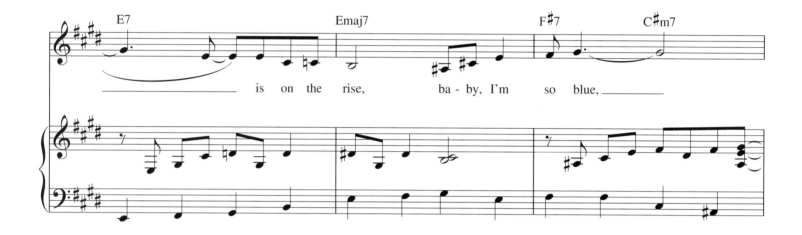

on _____ the way, ___ still I'm wait-in' all ___ in vain. _

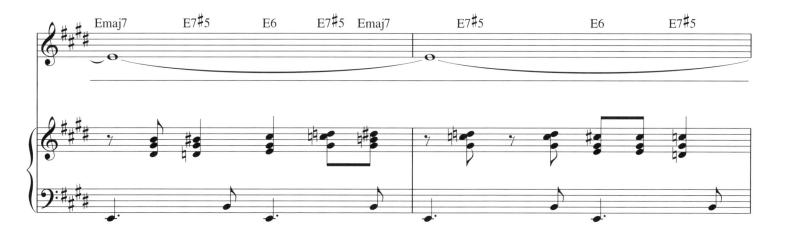

___ Should _ be ___ swing - in' down _ the lane ___ with you. _

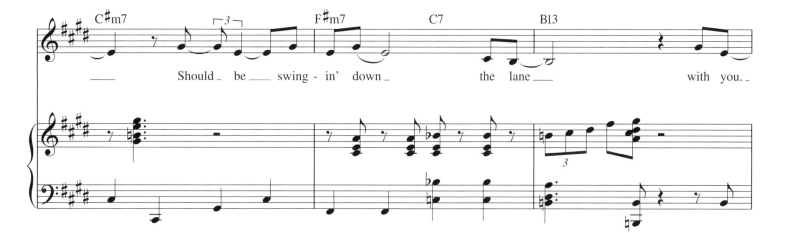

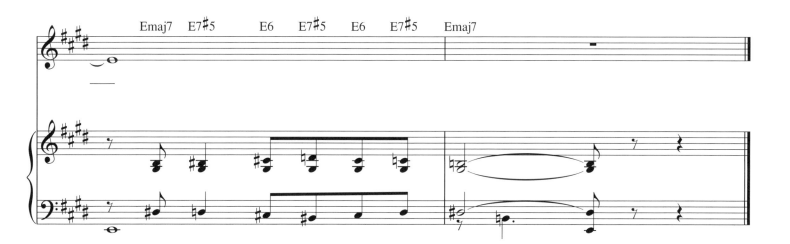

WAIT TILL YOU SEE HER
from BY JUPITER

Words by LORENZ HART
Music by RICHARD RODGERS

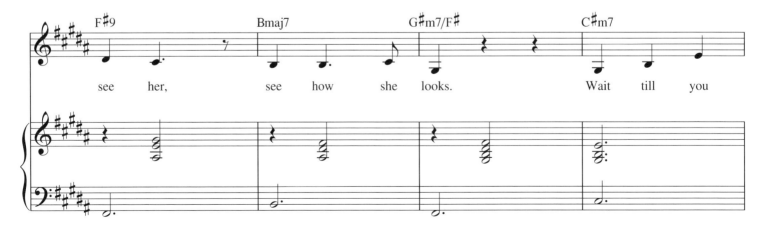

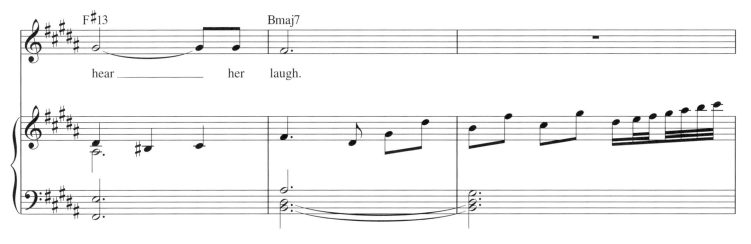

hear _____ her laugh.

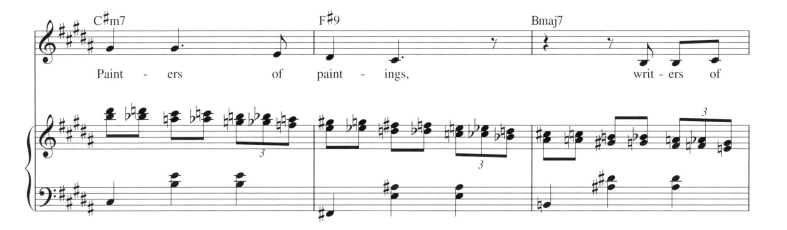

Paint - ers of paint - ings, writ - ers of

books, nev - er could tell _____ the half.

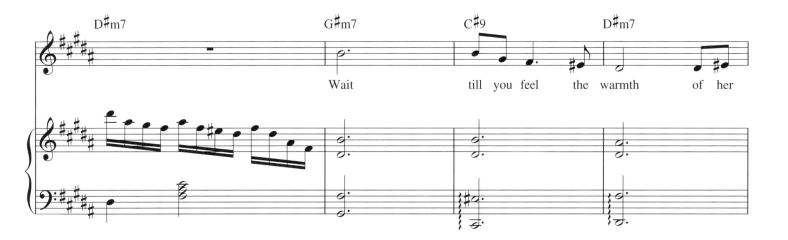

Wait till you feel the warmth of her

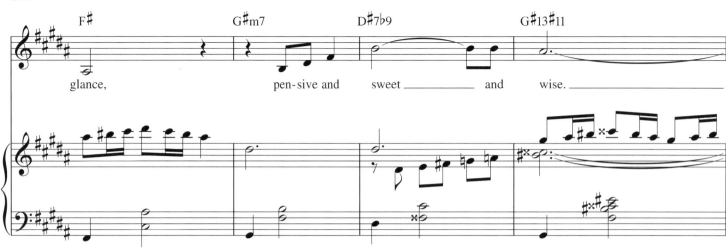

glance, pen-sive and sweet _____ and wise. _____

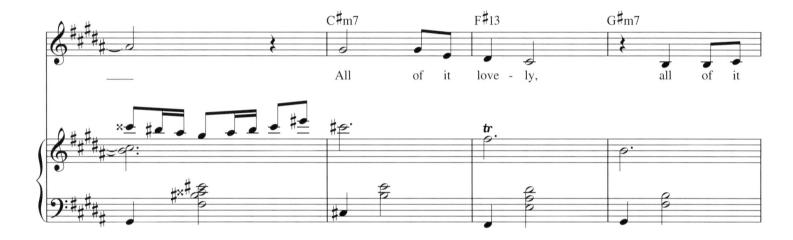

_____ All of it love - ly, all of it

thrill - ing. ___ I'll nev - er ___ be will - ing ___ to free

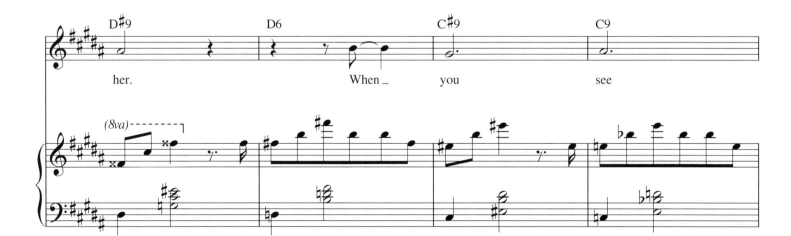

her. When ___ you see

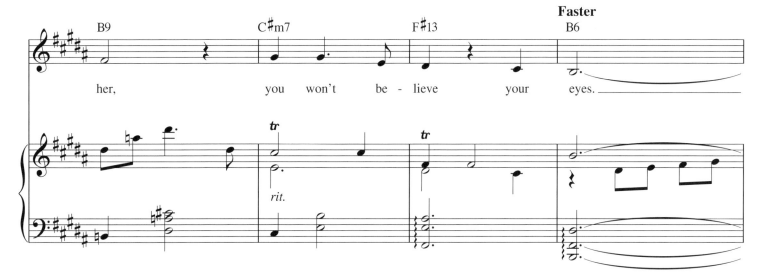

her, you won't be - lieve your eyes.

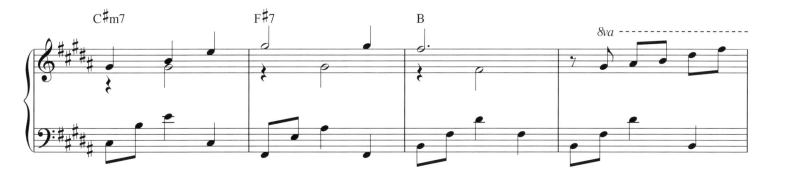

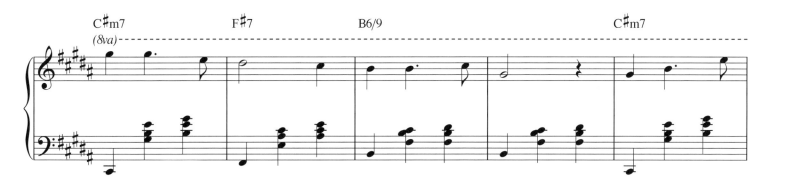

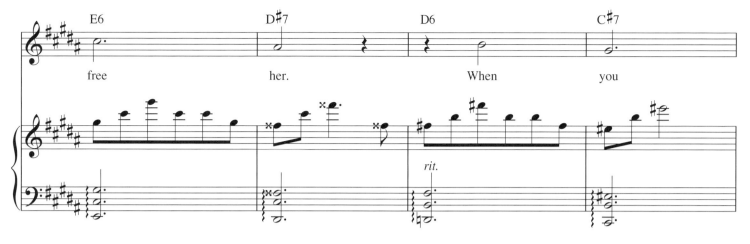

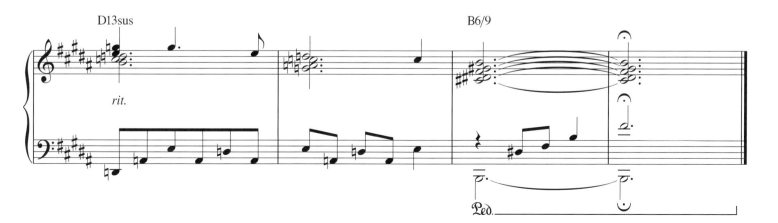

WHEN THE WORLD WAS YOUNG

English Lyric by JOHNNY MERCER
French Lyric by VANNIER
Music by M. PHILIPPE-GERARD

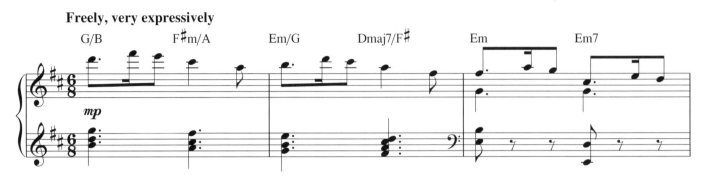

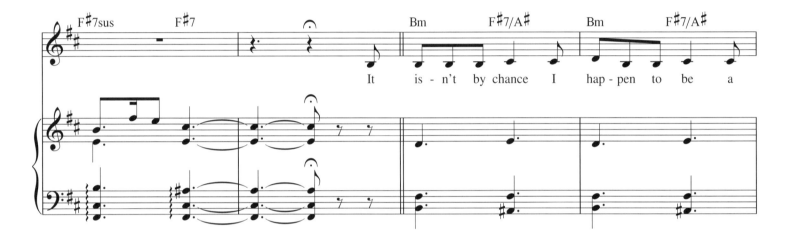

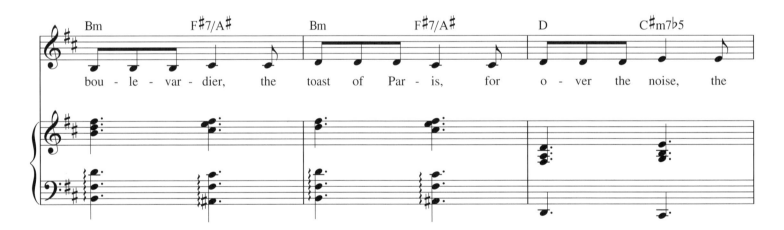

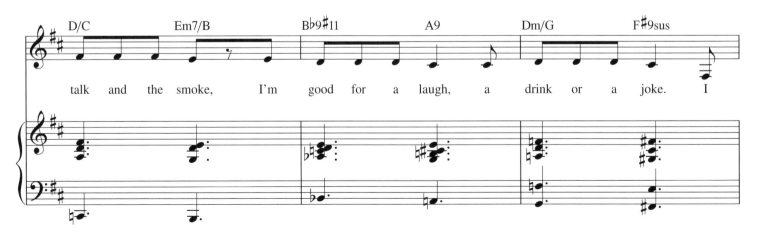

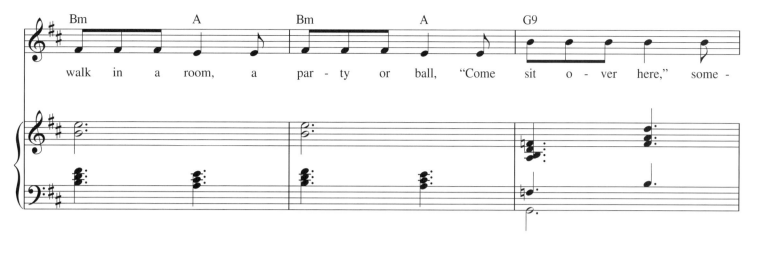

walk in a room, a par - ty or ball, "Come sit o - ver here," some -

bod - y will call. A drink for Mon - sieur, a drink for us all, but

how man - y times I stop and re - call:

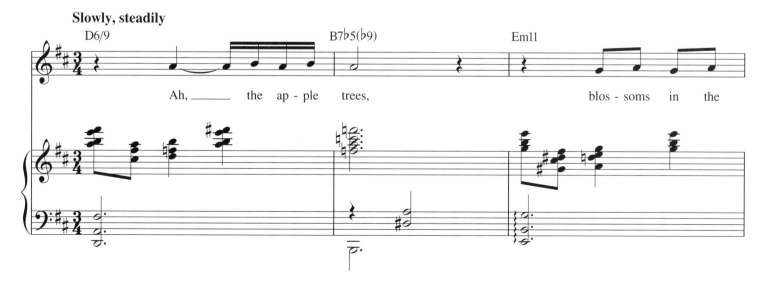

Slowly, steadily

Ah, ___ the ap - ple trees, blos - soms in the

breeze   that ____ we walked a - mong.

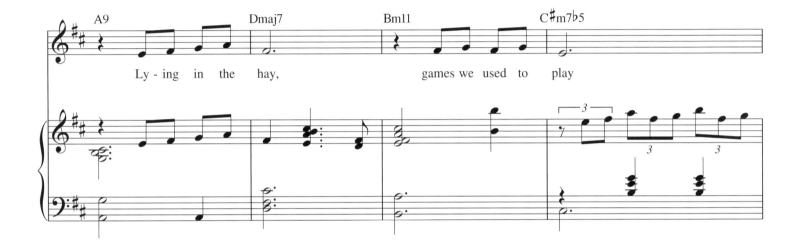

Ly - ing in the hay,   games we used to play

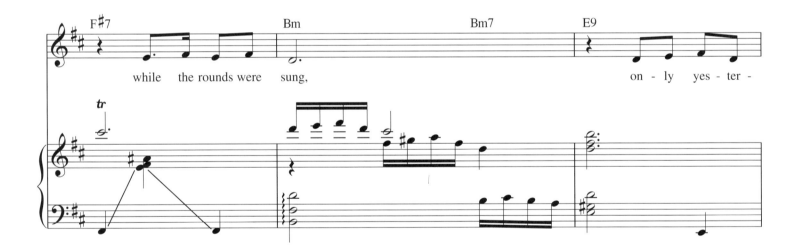

while the rounds were sung,   on - ly yes - ter -

day,   when the world was young.

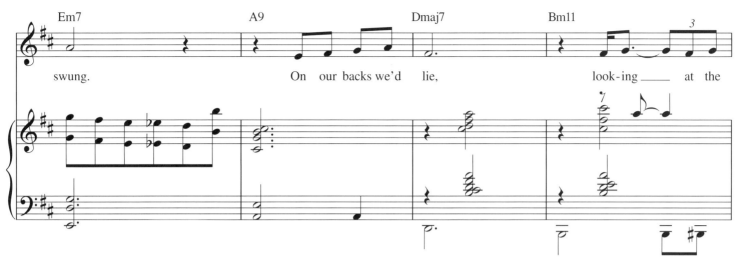

swung. On our backs we'd lie, look-ing____ at the

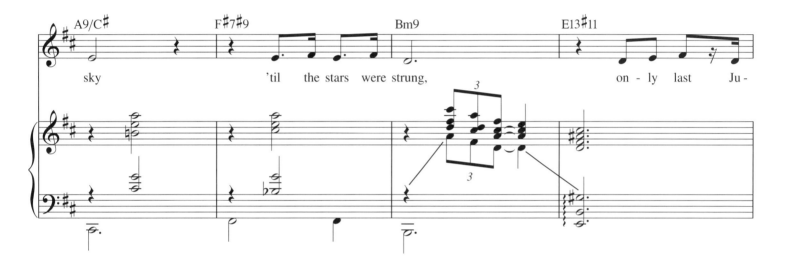

sky 'til the stars were strung, on - ly last Ju -

Slower

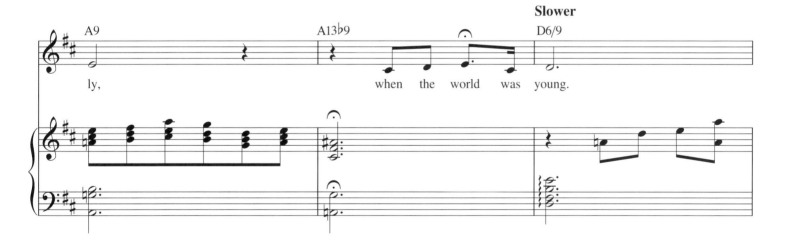

ly, when the world was young.

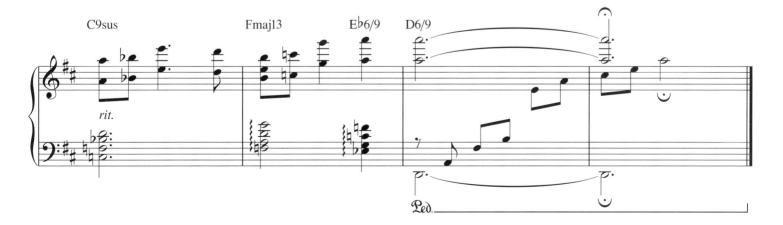

rit.

Ped.

YES INDEED

Words and Music by
SY OLIVER

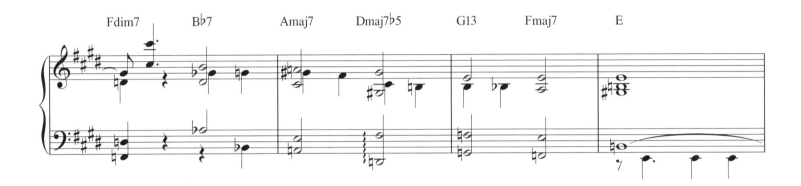

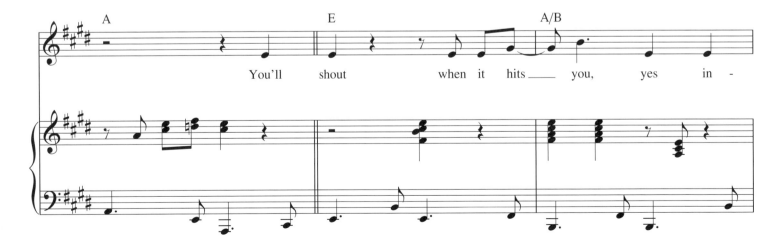

You'll shout when it hits ___ you, yes in -

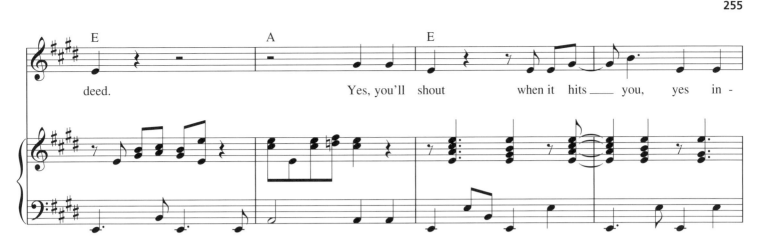

deed.   Yes, you'll shout   when it hits ___ you,   yes in -

deed.   When the spir - it moves you,   you'll

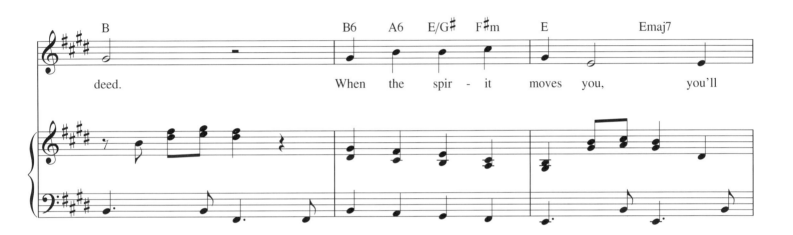

shout,   "Hal - le - lu - jah!"   When it hits _

___ you, _____ you'll hol - ler,   yes in - deed.

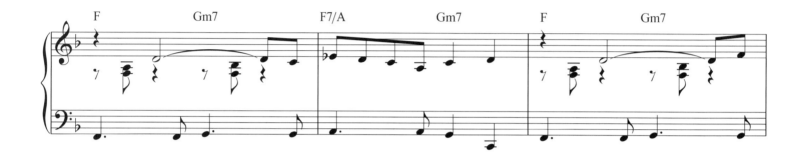

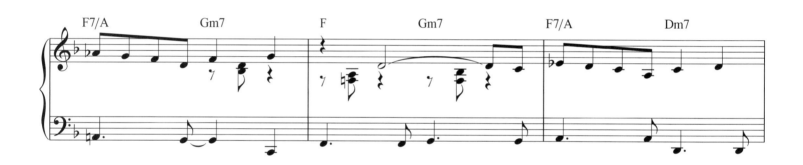

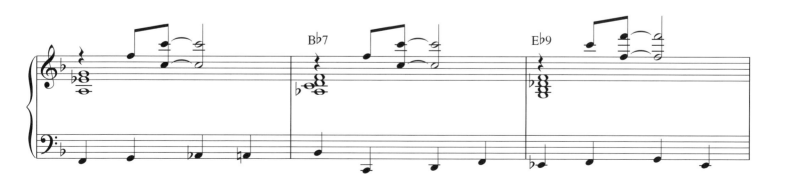

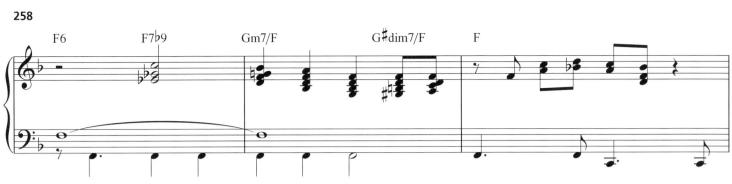

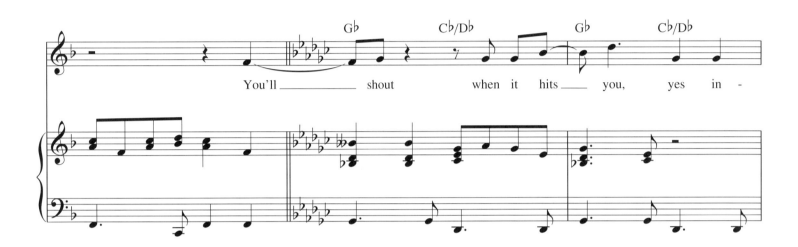

You'll _____ shout when it hits ____ you, yes in-

deed. Yes, you'll shout when it hits _

____ you, ____ yes in-deed. _____ When the spir - it

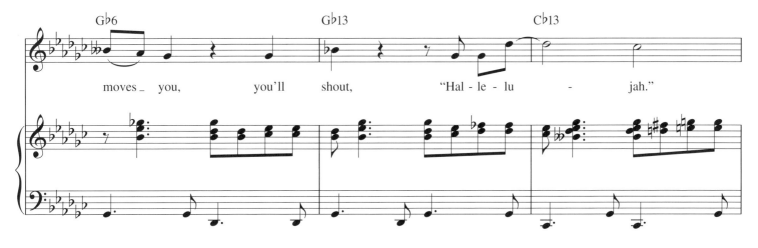

moves _ you, you'll shout, "Hal - le - lu - jah."

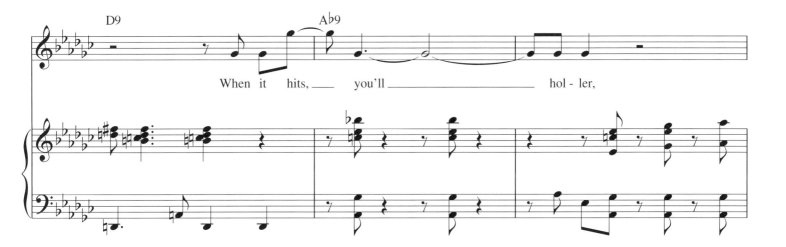

When it hits, ___ you'll _____ hol - ler,

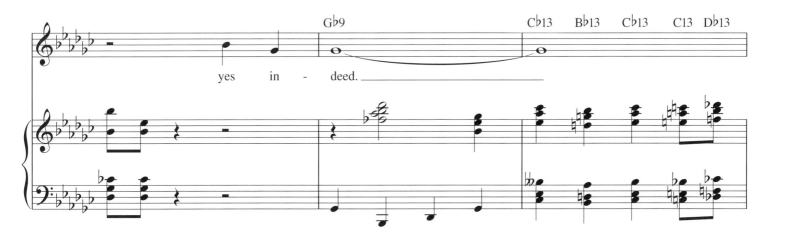

yes in - deed. _____

YOU'RE GETTING TO BE A HABIT WITH ME

Lyrics by AL DUBIN
Music by HARRY WARREN

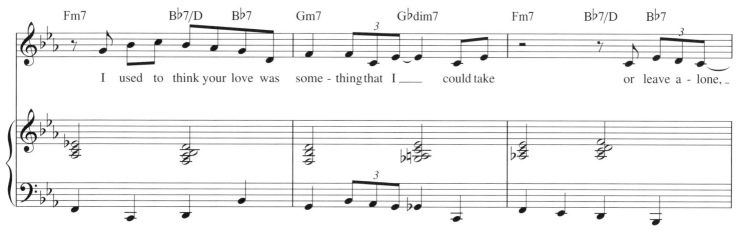

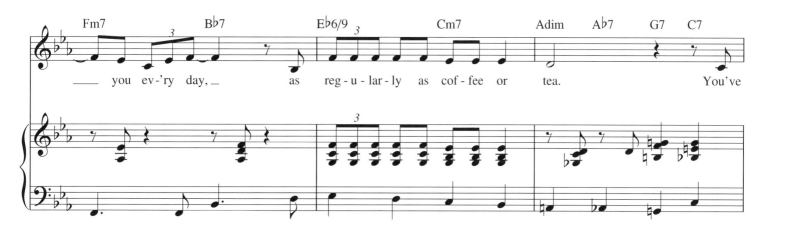

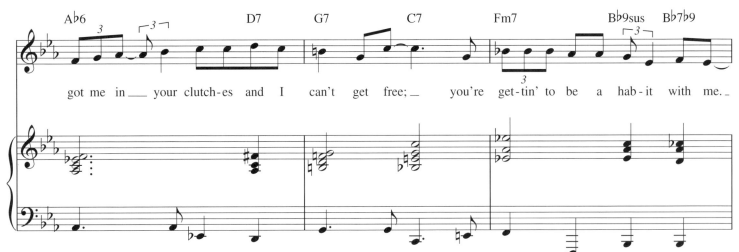

got me in ___ your clutch-es and I can't get free; ___ you're get-tin' to be a hab-it with me. ___

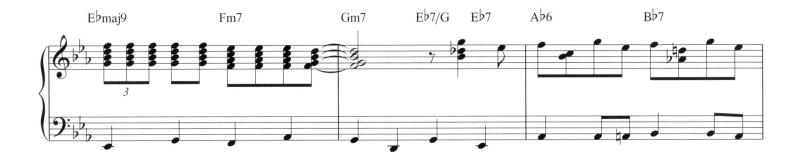

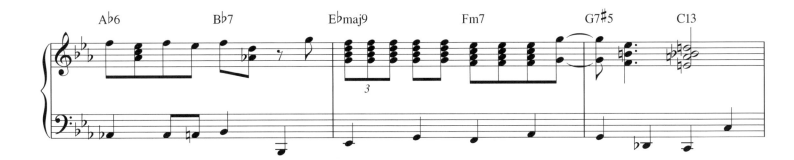

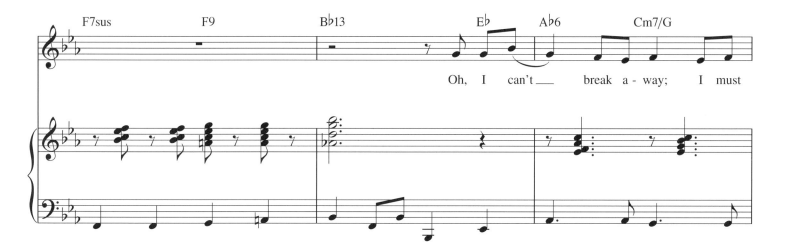

Oh, I can't __ break a - way; I must

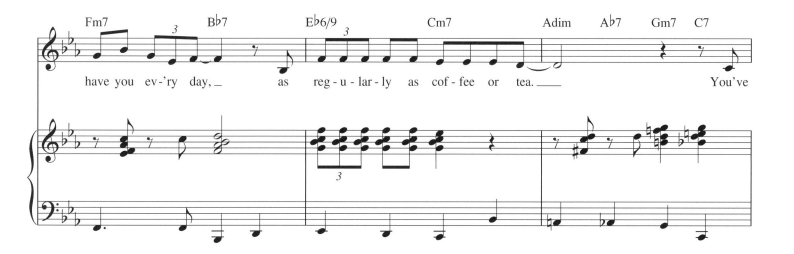

have you ev - 'ry day, __ as reg - u - lar - ly as cof - fee or tea. __ You've

got me in your clutch - es and I can't get free; _ you're get-tin' to be a hab-it with me. _

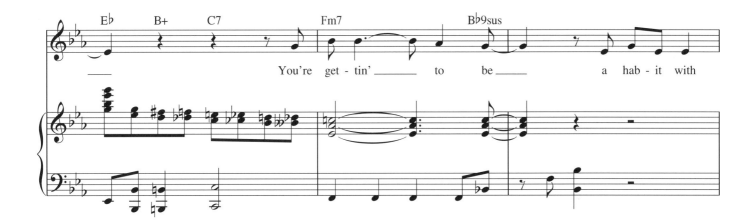

You're get - tin' _____ to be _____ a hab - it with

me.

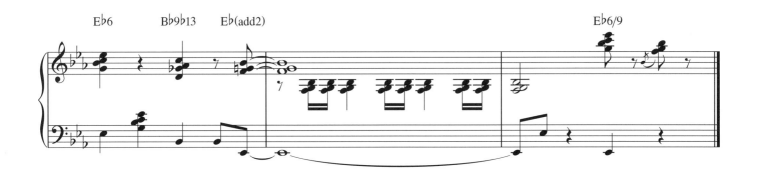